BestMasters

Springer awards “BestMasters” to the best application-oriented master’s theses, which were completed at renowned chairs of economic sciences in Germany, Austria, and Switzerland in 2013.
The works received highest marks and were recommended for publication by supervisors. As a rule, they show a high degree of application orientation and deal with current issues from different fields of economics.
The series addresses practitioners as well as scientists and offers guidance for early stage researchers.

Jeffry Straßer

Integrated Risk Management of Non-Maturing Accounts

Practical Application and Testing of a Dynamic Replication Model

Springer Gabler

Jeffry Straßer
Vienna, Austria

Masterthesis, University of Applied Sciences (bfi) Vienna, Austria

ISBN 978-3-658-04902-7 ISBN 978-3-658-04903-4 (eBook)
DOI 10.1007/978-3-658-04903-4

The Deutsche Nationalbibliothek lists this publication in the Deutsche Nationalbibliografie; detailed bibliographic data are available in the Internet at http://dnb.d-nb.de.

Library of Congress Control Number: 2014930568

Springer Gabler

Printed on acid-free paper

Springer Gabler is a brand of Springer DE.
Springer DE is part of Springer Science+Business Media.
www.springer-gabler.de

Foreword

The question how to value and manage specific banking products is one of the very central ones in risk management and asset & liability management in each bank. Particularly current accounts and sight deposits are very tricky to value and model due the simple fact that those products can be withdrawn - from a legal point of view - by customers at any time without notice but from an economic viewpoint are a relatively stable source of funding. The uncertainty of cash flows related to this withdrawal option by the customer on the one hand and the price flexibility in these products by banks on the other hand makes modelling those so called non-maturing accounts a challenge for risk and liquidity management.

The thesis of Mr. Straßer discusses the modelling of non-maturing accounts in a very innovative and technically elegant way. The method of dynamic modelling used by the author is based on stochastic simulation and optimization and is the latest development in this field. It is very likely that this method will replace the currently still widely used static modelling approach due to its flexibility and accuracy.

It is noteworthy that in the thesis a fully developed model is presented that can be implemented immediately without much adaptation for practical uses. The author demonstrates in a very precise way how varied sophisticated theoretical methods can be combined and being transformed into operatively useful models.

I congratulate Mr. Straßer on this excellent thesis and wish the reader a fascinating lecture with a lot of hints and suggestions for practical work.

Vienna, 11.10.2013
Manfred Dirngrabner

Contents

The graphs and charts in this book can be viewed with improved readability in colour online! Go to http://www.springer.com/ and look up the name of the author/title of the book to get access.

List of Figures

List of Tables

List of Appendices

List of Abbreviations

FTP	Funds Transfer Pricing
MMA	Money Market Account
MSP	Multistage Stochastic Program
NMA	Non-Maturing Account
NMD	Non-Maturing Deposit
NPV	Net Present Value
OLS	Ordinary Least Squares
OTS	Office of Thrift Supervision

Abstract

The modelling of customer accounts that neither have a fixed maturity nor a fixed interest rate remains a challenging yet necessary task in today's asset and liability management. The currently most elaborate dynamic modelling approach of such non-maturing accounts via a multistage stochastic program has not been subject to extensive empirical testing in different environments. Furthermore, practical recommendations for the implementation of this approach are scarce in scientific literature. This thesis outlines an implementation from scratch in detail using an open source statistical programming language and software. Modelling suggestions for all 3 main risk factors, market rates, client rates, and aggregated volumes are provided. Moreover, the chosen scenario generation procedure permits a fast and simple realization. A case study based on recent real savings account data supports the models expected superiority also in (after-)crisis times and for an individual bank product. In addition, it provides numerous tangible recommendations for model specifications derived from practical and mathematical consideration, as well as empirical findings.

1 Introduction

1.1 Topic and its Relevance

A considerable portion of a European commercial bank's balance sheet contains non-maturing client positions[1]. Their development is particularly hard to predict, as they have no contractually fixed conditions defining timing and volume of cash flows.

There is no market for derivatives to directly hedge the risks arising out of these non-maturing accounts (NMAs). Hence, to manage liquidity risk, interest rate risk and risk of changes in volumes of NMAs effectively, a valid modelling of these positions is crucial.

Furthermore, a unit of volume of an NMA has a potential positive net present value (NPV), e.g. due to client rates paid for demand deposits that are lower than the bank's discount rate. To encourage this possibly cheap funding, banks also set internal funds transfer prices of NMAs to provide optimal incentives for their acquisition and the internal distribution of these funds.

Next to these internal reasons, a bank needs proper risk modelling to satisfy changing regulatory requirements. More sophisticated but reasonable modelling that shows empirical improvements in its effectiveness should positively influence the regulating authorities' demands.

Finally, determining an economic value of NMAs is frequently discussed with respect to accounting and taxation purposes.

Currently, most banks apply static replication models that use one historical scenario only[2]. These models attempt to replicate the past behaviour of an NMA by a portfolio of plain vanilla market instruments and use it for (future) risk management. In the last two decades rapidly changing financial markets and financial crises revealed shortcomings of this approach. Therefore, research towards models that incorporate statistical information, economic reasoning, as well as the stochastic nature of relevant explanatory variables has been intensified.

---

[1]E.g. Sight and savings deposits account for more than 35% of total domestic liabilities of Austria's four biggest banking groups in 2011. See Österreichische Nationalbank (2012).

[2]See Blöchlinger (2011), p. 3; Frauendorfer/Schürle (2007), p. 330

Practitioners in medium-sized commercial banking groups in general neither have experience with state-of-the-art dynamic models as they are proposed in scientific literature nor the abilities or resources to start the development of such a model from scratch. Therefore, this thesis provides an introduction of already developed models as well as a case study on how to handle a first implementation of a sophisticated model framework with reasonable time and effort, using the statistical programming language R[3] and spreadsheet software.

The results are compared with a static model in a case study with real savings account data and support previous findings of superiority[4]. Furthermore, numerous different model settings are applied and recommendations for the practical use are derived.

1.2 Formulating the Research Questions

Did multistage stochastic programming models perform better than a static model in the past, in terms of margin level and margin stability?
Which model specifications are most suitable in practice?

1.3 State of the Literature

The topic of valuing NMAs has been brought forward in scientific literature in the last two decades, and is still a very controversial one. Theoretically, many different kinds of models and model specifications have been developed to value, measure the inherent risks, and hedge NMAs. However, empirical studies about those models are scarce, above all because of the lack of data, data quality and the cumbersome implementation. Most empirical studies analyse aggregated data of the banking sector in specific countries as they are disclosed by national banks. Moreover, they are concentrated to US data (with recent exceptions), although the topic might be even more important for Continental-Europe economies, which are comparably more bank-intermediated[5]. Hence, conclusions from those studies for applications in single European banks have to be drawn with special care, because the differences among individual banks are huge even in the same economy[6]. Chapter 2 recaps the state of literature in detail.

---

[3] R Development Core Team (2008).

[4] Frauendorfer/Schürle (2007), pp. 353-355

[5] Dewachter et al. (2006), p. 9

[6] See Hutchison/ Pennacchi (1996), pp. 399-417 or O'Brien (2000), pp. 1-44 for empirical evidence.

1.4 Methodological Approach

Extensive literature research and discussions with practitioners build the theoretical basis for this thesis.

The main part incorporates quantitative data analysis tools and models such as term structure models, econometric models and optimization procedures, which are applied in the statistical programming language R as well as in spreadsheet software.

Secondary market data is collected from public websites and commercial data providers, and used for model calibration along with internal data from a Euro zone based bank.

Validation via performance analysis, benchmarking and critical interpretation of the results complete the case study.

1.5 Structure of the Thesis

Chapter 1 gives an introduction on the thesis topic. Chapter 2 depicts the practical uses and economic necessity of modelling non-maturing accounts in banks. Furthermore, it gives an overview of existing literature and outlines the basic concepts and assumptions behind the model applied in the thesis. Each main risk factor that is taken into account in the model is then explained in detail in chapter 3, including modelling and calibration approaches as well as data sample describtions. Subsequently, chapter 4 puts the risk factors in a dynamic simulation framework, and shows how to find the optimal model output. Chapter 5 deals with model outputs of a case study and makes comparisons between different models and specifications. Furthermore the outcomes are critically assessed, and a validation of the model is attempted. Finally, chapter 6 concludes on the findings and gives an outlook for the future.

1.6 Definitions and Assumptions

The thesis incorporates a number of different models that build on several theoretical assumptions:

The term structure model is based on the "Fundamental Theorem of Asset Pricing" and the "Pricing Rule Presentation Theorem" which together assume the[7]:

- Absence of arbitrage

---

[7] Dybvig/Ross (1987), pp. 100-106

- Existence of an optimal demand for some agent who prefers more to less
- Existence of a linear pricing rule;
- Existence of a risk-neutral probability measure (the martingale property)[8]
- Existence of a state price density

Furthermore, a complete market[9] is assumed.

The calibration and use of the regression types applied for modelling client rate and NMA volumes, assume certain distributions of the error terms that might not necessarily be true for the data sample.

Additionally, there are several other assumed economic relations that explain empirical correlations and model coefficients, which will be elaborated on later in the thesis.

Finally, certain assumptions about data distributions in particular normal distributions are implicit in the framework and will be pointed out.

---

[8] For further information see Duffie (2001), pp. 101-128

[9] A market is complete, if every payoff for any future state-of-the-world can be constructed by a portfolio of existing assets without friction (see Flood (1991), pp. 35-36).

2 Analysing the Practical Problem

One of the major businesses and purposes of a bank is to act as an intermediary between savers and investors[10]. It collects deposits on the one side and issues loans on the other side. Thus, a main source of income is the interest rate difference between interest paid to savers on the one hand and received from borrowers on the other hand.

The bank earns money not only due to the intermediary service that it provides, but for taking on several risks. Thereof the most important are credit default risk, interest rate risk and liquidity risk. The latter two are, at least in part, arising from term transformation. Term transformation or "structural position" refers to the fact that liabilities tend to have much lower durations than assets in a bank's balance sheet[11]. This can be explained by the market demand for long term asset products like loans and short term liability products like transaction and savings accounts.

The major aim of asset and liability management (ALM) is to manage the interest rate risk and liquidity risk arising due to the mentioned differences and mismatches in the balance sheet structure[12].

However, creating a sound framework for ALM is not a trivial task, because certain products (NMAs) exhibit the special feature of having no contractual maturity, which means that cash flows can occur at any time, or only require a short time of notice. On the liability side sight deposits, money market deposits, and savings deposits are among others typical products of that type. On the asset side these products are less numerous, but exist in the form of credit card loans, overdrafts and in some cases loans with prepayment options.

In return for the client's freedom of choice regarding timing and amount of the cash flows of these products, the bank reserves the right to adjust interest rates of existing contracts and also makes use of this possibility.

On the one hand, reasons for changes in those client rates may be strategic, such as raising rates relative to competitors in order to keep deposits longer and attract more volume. On the other hand, rate adjustments are due to changes in the

---

[10] Llewellyn (1999), p. 9

[11] Bessis (2010), p. 274

[12] Bessis (2010), p. 268

current market situation, in other words the current interest rate level or yield curve.

Due to absence of direct hedging instruments for NMAs, they need to be modelled to be manageable. This can be done by fitting a replicating portfolio[13] of fixed-income securities to either the expected present values and their interest rate sensitivity of NMAs or other optimization approaches with interest rates, client rates and volumes as major input factors. This portfolio may then be integrated in the ALM process and used to derive hedging and structural decisions as well as expected profit margins from it.

Moreover, as non-maturing accounts serve as funding for longer term asset products, their aggregate internal valuation or pricing becomes important. The term funds transfer pricing (FTP) stands for the rate that is paid internally to units of the bank that acquire the funds and that are charged for providing funds to asset side units, which e.g. give out loans. The bank's internal intermediary function is usually taken by the treasury department. The calculated FTP should give the profit-maximizing incentive for raising deposits[14].

Furthermore, to follow an integrated risk management approach, this model should take liquidity risks into account, which arise from a possible decline of NMA volumes.

Finally, for accounting and taxation reasons, one may be interested in the economic value of NMAs. However, under the current legislation (IFRS) it is prohibited, to account for economic values of NMAs in financial statements, therefore the emphasis lies on the other purposes outlined above.

2.1 Expectations and Uses for the Model

The requirements for such a model are numerous. It has to reflect the complex real situation of the development in non-maturing accounts cash flows in an accurate way. This is difficult, as there is a wide range of possible influencing factors like market interest rates, macro-economic developments, political or environmental events, corporation specific events, and finally always human behaviour and reasoning.

[13] This hedging approach is a widely used technique in most scientific papers on that topic and will be an integrated part in the model used in this thesis.

[14] Sheehan (2004), p. 1

Apart from finding a causally correct model, the output of such a model must be sufficiently practical, so that users will be able to deduct business or hedging decisions from it.

In practise, the model has to be easy to use, easy to maintain, compatible with standard business IT-systems in banking environment, and implementation should require only a minimum necessary amount of resources. That implies a certain degree of simplicity and an efficient implementation into the IT-landscape of the bank.

Furthermore the model must be able to deal with available data, and data quality. This is a special topic in practise and in theory, as empirical studies are rather scarce in literature, and data samples usually comprise aggregate data published by central banks or specific product groups of individual banks. Therefore, a model that worked in such a case study doesn't have to be eligible for generalization.

Additionally, as risk management is mainly a forward-looking task, the model should rather simulate future scenarios than reflecting one past scenario only.

However, if a proper model for pricing of NMAs and timing of NMA cash flows can be found, hedging should be made possible with existing financial products.

2.2 Approaches in Literature and Banking Practise

Valuation and risk management of non-maturing accounts is a young topic in scientific literature. Generally speaking, all models currently suggested deal to some extent with the following three risk factors and their interrelations:

1. Market interest rates
2. Client rate paid on the NMA
3. Volume of the NMA

Although possibly crucial factors, macro variables are generally neglected[15], due to the lack of frequent, timely and reliable data and even more sophisticated and still poorly performing forecasting models[16] for macroeconomic figures.

This thesis concerns itself with dynamic replication models. The term "dynamic" indicates that the three risk factors mentioned above are simulated in numerous scenarios and do not rely on only one historical scenario. Furthermore, it alludes to

[15] With exceptions: e.g. O'Brien (2000).

[16] Kalkbrener, M., Willing (2004), p. 1566

the model's capability of considering future changes in the composition of the replicating portfolio, whereas a static model assumes the same composition at all time.

The following chart (Figure 1) gives an overview on the concepts of NMA valuation and risk management models that make use of market rates (r), client rates (cr), and NMA volumes (V).

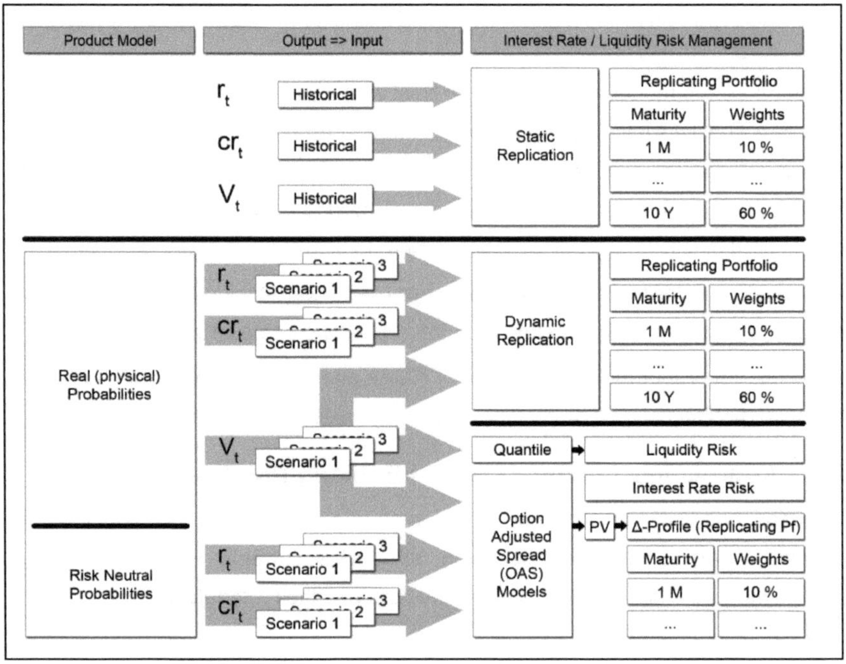

Figure 1: Overview of Static and Dynamic Models for NMA management[17]

A static replication model serves as a benchmark in a case study of this thesis. OAS models first implement a formula to calculate a NPV for the NMA, which is afterwards tested for interest rate sensitivity. From the resulting (interest rate) risk profile a replicating portfolio with the same risk profile can be generated. Liquidity risk then has to be treated separately. In this thesis no OAS model is implemented. Nevertheless, the important input and progress they brought for dynamic replication models are included in the following chronological literature overview.

[17] Heidorn/Schmaltz (2008), p. 161

An early approach by the Office of Thrift Supervision[18] (OTS) uses discounted expected cash flows to value NMAs and examine their interest rate sensitivity. The OTS calculates present values for different yield curve scenarios, without accounting for possible influences on client rates or NMA volumes. The major deficiency of this approach are deterministic functions for client rates paid, deposit volume evolution and market rates[19], while the latter two are widely assumed to be at least partly stochastic in nature. Also the revised version of their framework[20] remains similarly simplistic.

O'Brien, Orphanides and Small[21], introduce a stochastic valuation framework that values NMAs and durations of the NPV in a Monte Carlo simulation from a risk neutral view. However, this might be misleading, given that market agents are at least in some situations risk averse.

Selvaggio[22] adds no-arbitrage arguments to his stochastic valuation framework.

Hutchison and Pennacchie[23] adopt an equilibrium-based valuation approach, accounting for market imperfections of bank liabilities[24] and incorporating a square-root, mean reverting interest rate process.

One major approach for the valuation of NMAs which has been used by many subsequent (OAS) models in literature has been brought forward by Jarrow and van Deventer[25] (1998). In their paper they introduce a framework for valuing NMAs based on imperfect markets and no arbitrage arguments. A net present value of future cash flows is derived using a risk-neutral valuation procedure[26]. However, this implies the strong underlying assumption of a complete market. The authors therefore assume for simplicity that the variables for NMA volume and client rates

[18] Office of Thrift Supervision (1994)

[19] Jarrow/van Deventer (1998), pp. 251

[20] Office of Thrift Supervision (2001)

[21] O'Brien et.al.(1994), pp. 400-435

[22] Selvaggio (1996), pp. 363-373

[23] Hutchison/Pennacchi (1996), pp. 399-417

[24] This is the first model that claims to use a so-called general contingent claims framework. This alludes to the application of option-pricing theory (see Black/Scholes (1973), pp. 637-654) to any asset whose value depends on one or several "state variables" of possible relevant future states of the economy. For an elaboration on contingent claims, see Elliott/Kopp (1999), p. 2.

[25] Jarrow/van Deventer (1998), pp. 249-272

[26] No-Arbitrage Theory combined with a complete market assumption allows deriving a unique martingale measure that converts all discounted asset prices into martingales. The basis for this theory, assumptions and the mathematical derivation the risk neutral measure can be found in

for NMAs depend only on the term structure evolution deducted from treasury securities[27].

Furthermore, they show that the payoff using their formula resembles an exotic[28] interest rate swap with variable notional, which may be hedged by investing in bonds with different maturities (replicating portfolio).

Jarrow and van Deventer adopt previous approaches with regards to risk factors: A term structure model provides a scenario for the future (short-term) market rate, while client rate and deposit volumes are deterministic functions thereof.

A subsequent empirical analysis of by Janosi, Jarrow, and Zulli[29] shows a consistence with previous studies and promotes the validity of the model.

O'Brien[30] shows a way to account for deposit rate stickiness and asymmetric deposit rate adjustments[31]. This asymmetry leads to different interest rate sensitivities in case of positive or negative market rate shocks. He adds the level of income and a random error term as explanatory variables for deposit balances and another random error term to the client rate equation. Moreover, he expresses doubts that simple autoregressive models are valid for representing deposit premiums in a distant future.

De Jong and Wielhouwer examine particularly "the effects of the dynamic adjustment of the interest paid on the account and balance"[32], while taking the market rate evolution as an exogenous variable. They use an error-correction model[33]for deviations from long term means of NMA volume and add the spread between a money market account (MMA) and the rate paid on the NMA as a variable to the their framework.

An intuitively reasonable specification of the methodology behind a term structure model for that kind of application has been first suggested by Kalkbrener and

---

[27] The assumption of a unique equivalent risk measure should only be made when using a term structure model with only one stochastic factor that follows the short rate. Using multi-factor models requires to derive an equivalent risk measure by other means (eg.: Schweizer 1995, pp. 1-32

[28] "Exotic" refers in this case not only to the possibly increasing or decreasing notional, but also to the swap of two variable rates, client rate for market interest rate in particular.

[29] Janosi et al. (1999), pp. 8-31

[30] O'Brien (2000), pp. 1-44

[31] Chapter 3.2 will elaborate on these concepts.

[32] De Jong/Wielhouwer (2003), pp. 384

[33] For more information on error-correction models see Davidson et al. (1978), pp 661-692

Willing[34]. They state that a calibration of the parameters should be done on a set of past data, rather than from current market values of plain vanilla instruments. This is due to the intention of forecasting realistic interest rates for a longer period of time (several years), whereas the usual goal is to price rather short-term derivatives.

They propose a deterministic client rate function, with dependency on market rates of different maturities. Furthermore, they use a stochastic term in their volume function, as they didn't find much correlation between market rates and NMA[35] volumes in their case study that would explain the volume evolution with sufficient accuracy. To account for liquidity risk, they introduce a quantile measure of the outcomes from a Monte Carlo simulation using their volume model.

A multistage stochastic programming methodology for the valuation of NMAs was published by Frauendorfer and Schürle[36] in 2003 (after previous publications on that topic[37]). This refers to an optimization technique, which takes into account that decisions can be made in several points in time throughout the valuation or calibration period. In particular the weights of a replicating portfolio may be changed at each stage. This makes the model dynamic as compared to a static one, where the weights of the replicating portfolio are the same for the whole period. Their quite intuitive reasoning for the necessity of changing weights is the development of the environment (changing market rates, client behaviour, etc.) and its effects on the cash flow pattern of the NMA.

Their empirical case study showed an "improvement"[38] in model performance measured by either standard deviation or return (profit margin) figures. This was consistent with practical experience by a major Swiss bank, which had applied the model in practise for several years.

Sheehan[39] puts the focus on analysing the development of current volumes without new business (retained balances) of NMAs, stating that early works that

---

[34] Kalkbrener/Willing (2004), pp. 1547-1568

[35] In their paper they focus on deposit accounts such as demand deposits, saving accounts, and short time deposits.

[36] Frauendorfer/Schürle (2003), pp. 602-616

[37] Schürle (1998), pp. 1; Frauendorfer/Schürle (2000), pp. 67-101; Frauendorfer/Schürle (2000), pp. 189-209

[38] Improvement in this case, stands for a higher average margin, while causing less model violations in the form of refinancing activities.

[39] Sheehan (2004), pp. 1-34

use total balances do not capture the real interest rate sensitivity. Furthermore he questions the complete market assumption for the lending market and incorporates a lending market equation in his valuation model. He proves that the treasury rate (as a reference for the short rate) serves as a lower bound for the client rate.

Fidelity premiums[40], as they are common in the Benelux states, have been incorporated in the valuation model by Laurent[41]. Her findings include that a fidelity premium that raises the total interest paid to the client above the short-term discount rate might still result in a positive NPV of the NMA. Her work is particularly interesting in the current environment, where stable deposits are an integrated part in the Basel III liquidity coverage ratio[42]. With her specifications the model might be able to provide sufficient reason for regulatory reporting on that matter.

In the course of designing more profound regulations in the banking sector, the Basel Committee introduced "Principles for the Management and Supervision of Interest Rate Risk"[43]. This rather rough framework explicitly mentions simulation approaches that may "involve assumptions about a bank's strategy for changing administered interest rates[44] [...], about the behaviour of the bank's customers [...], and/or about the future stream of business"[45]. That recommendation aims for capturing option-like payoff structures in a bank's balance sheet, but it also clearly indicates, that the Basel Committee is aware of already implemented and functioning models in practise. However, the state of scientific literature might not entirely reflect the progressiveness of models that may had existed by the time of the release of this principles and have been developed by now in banking practise, primarily by large sophisticated international banking groups.

Dewachter, Lyrio, and Maes[46] incorporate no-arbitrage multifactor flexible-affine term structure models[47] into their framework, which generate a better fit to

---

[40] This term refers to an extra remuneration on top of the base client rate for deposits that remain in the clients account for an extended period of time, e.g. longer than a year.

[41] Laurent (2004), pp. 1-27

[42] Basel Committee on Banking Supervision (2010), pp. 12-13

[43] Basel Committee on Banking Supervision (2004), pp. 1-40

[44] Administered rate products are a synonym for NMAs in the scope of this thesis.

[45] Basel Committee on Banking Supervision (2004), p. 30

[46] Dewachter et al. (2006), pp. 1-39

historical data as well as more realistic future yield curve dynamics. They suggest including future expected deposits only if "they can be identified in a verifiable way"[48]. However, due to lack of data, they run their model several times assuming different decay rates of existing balances and one constant balance case.

Bardenhewer[49] provides a theoretical overview of NMA models with a special focus on the risk management purpose. He describes a methodology for constructing a replicating portfolio, based on moving averages of market rates[50]. Additionally, he answers important questions that might confuse the risk management practitioner regarding assumptions and specifications of the model.

In 2007 Frauendorfer and Schürle[51] published a comprehensive framework for NMA valuation, by extending their multistage stochastic programming model from 2003 with detailed descriptions of risk factor models and a more tangible explanation of their methodology. They use a two-factor extended Vasicek model for the term structure evolution, a threshold model for client rates with stepwise changes, and a third stochastic factor for their deposit balance equation.

An extensive empirical study of NMAs among German banks, including a wide range of different model specifications with respect to the term structure model (TSM) and the client rate model has been carried out by Entrop et al.[52].Holding the NMA balances constant in their simulations, they conclude that:

- For assessing the NPV of the NMA, the choice of either TSM or pass-through model is of minor importance. Hence, less sophisticated model specifications can be used for simplicity and easy implementation.
- For assessing interest rate risk of the NMA it is important to use an elaborate TSM and an appropriate bank-specific pass-through model.

As this thesis is focused on the latter, it indicates the necessity of a sophisticated model approach.

---

47 ""Multifactor" refers to more than 1 stochastic factor. "Flexible-affine" alludes to possible changes in the market prices of risk. An example and evidence of superiority of such a model has been shown by Dai and Singleton (2000), pp. 1943-1978.

48 Dewachter et al. (2006), p. 8. They give an example of a required deposit account for the salary of a customer that takes out a long-term mortgage from the bank.

49 Bardenhewer (2007), pp. 220-256.

50 The idea of this approach was provided by Wilson (1994).

51 Frauendorfer/Schürle (2007), pp. 327-359

52 Entrop et al. (2009), pp. 1-38

Paraschiv and Schürle introduce an elaborate model for client rate and NMA volumes in 2010[53]. They incorporate a threshold error-correction model by deriving an equilibrium client rate from the co-integration[54] of market and client rates. Additionally, they take a long term market rate into account, whereas previous models used only one short term rate as explanatory variable. Their volume model uses amongst others a lagged spread between client rate and a weighted rate of a short and a long term market rate, which is also a new approach.

Recent literature attempts to enrich current models by adding behavioural aspects. Nyström[55] describes a modelling approach that incorporates a customer's option to shift money between a low rate transaction account and higher rate savings accounts. To take into account individual and possibly irrational behaviour he defines the concept of customer specific strike prices for exercising their options, which he models on an aggregate basis via a certain strike price distribution. The option is exercised, when it is exceeded by "certain stochastic processes, which depend on the market rate, the deposit rates on the accounts as well as the amounts already deposited."[56]

Moreover, his deposit rate process is a function of the market rate and deposit balances, which reflects a bank's strategy to reward higher balances of single customers.

Blöchlinger[57] suggests an approach that integrates the banks marketing strategy into the hedging model. Instead of deriving the client rate by a regression model from market rates, he proposes a direct modelling of a banks pricing strategy in the form of a jump process. He therefore promotes a close cooperation between ALM and sales departments as an update of the rate function is required whenever the pricing strategy changes. When it comes to hedging, he claims that only cash flows after subtracting a profit margin should be replicated, since a portfolio of arbitrage-free instruments cannot possibly replicate cash flows that include excess returns.

---

[53] Paraschiv/Schürle (2010), pp. 1-24

[54] For further Information on Co-Integration see Engle/Granger (1987), pp.251-276

[55] Nyström (2008), pp.709-756

[56] Nyström (2008), pp. 754

[57] Blöchlinger (2011), pp. 1-47.

Paraschiv and Frauendorfer[58] provide an up-to-date overview of elaborate client rate and NMA volume approaches, including empirical case studies with Swiss national bank data.

2.3 Implications for the Model

To recap on the findings of previous studies on NMA modelling, this sub-chapter summarises all the implications for a model that serves the described purposes.

The model fulfils the requirements of:

- Reflecting the complex reality accurately
- Using only available data
- Having clearly stated assumptions, that are taken into account when the results are interpreted and business decisions are made
- Incorporating functions for all necessary uncertain variables that have a major impact on the value and interest rate sensitivity of an NMA
- Including a term structure model that provides valid outputs for an extended period of time (up to 10 years, to capture most of the relevant cash flows[59]) also for longer term spot rates
- Incorporating a client rate equation that reflects the internal pricing strategy of NMAs accurately
- Incorporating an NMA volume equation that is appropriate for the respective NMA product
- An estimation of acquisition and servicing costs of NMAs, net of fees paid by depositors
- "A theoretically sound method of discounting, either discounting expected cash flows at a risk-adjusted rate or discounting certainty-equivalent cash flows at a riskless rate"[60].
- Sound calibration techniques based on relevant data for the specific bank
- Being implementable into standard IT systems

[58] Paraschiv/Frauendorfer (2011), pp. 1-56.

[59] Dewachter et al. (2006), p. 16.

[60] Ellis/Jordan (2001), pp. 12.

2.4 Applied Model

Regulators yet did not recommend using any particular method for valuation and risk management of NMAs, but rather try to raise awareness of the strong assumptions the different models are based on[61]. As a result, models in practise are either rather simplistic or differ quite substantially among each other, reflecting ideas of practitioners in individual banks and their interpretations of scientific literature.

This thesis is based on currently one of the most sophisticated models on this topic suggested by Frauendorfer and Schürle[62]: A multistage stochastic programming technique to derive a replicating portfolio.

The setup of the multistage stochastic program strongly resembles the one proposed in their paper from 2007. However, all three main risk factor models are re-examined under consideration of other ideas in literature and new empirical findings. A trade-off is made between the most realistic modelling and easy implementation.

An overview of the concept and the single steps in this model is given now (excluding the necessary data process in practise):

1. As a starting point, a term structure model will be specified and set-up. As the other risk factors correlate or depend on its outcomes, this model should be chosen with special care. However, this is already one of the most complex tasks when it comes to the implementation of a calibration process.
2. A client rate model has to be developed and calibrated, which is, amongst other explanatory variables, a function of one or more market rates modelled in step 1.
3. The NMA volume evolution has to be considered by an appropriate model. This step is strongly interrelated with the previous one, as NMA volumes might influence client rates and vice versa. That is why a chronological order is not clear-cut here, but existing models in literature widely assume the causality to be as depicted here.

---

[61] See Ellis/Jordan (2001), pp. 4, and Basel Committee on Banking Supervision (2009), pp. 56-58.

[62] Frauendorfer/Schürle (2007), pp. 327-359

4. In the next step, the risk factor models are put into a scenario simulation framework: A valid method for creating a small amount of future paths that are representative for the uncertainty assumed in the risk factor models needs to be applied. In this thesis the approach of an approximation of the continuous distributions via a multinomial distribution is chosen. After each stage a scenario set is created describing future paths of the risk factors. As this scenario set is added to each of the previous outcomes, the result is a scenario tree with an exponentially rising number of nodes for each new stage. As a consequence, the number of scenarios per scenario set needs to be kept as small as possible to guarantee implementability[63].
5. An optimization is then performed over all stages on an objective criterion, e.g. minimizing the absolute deviation from the NMA costs plus a margin or just a maximization of the overall income over the simulation period. Unconditional probabilities are used to weight scenarios and a proper formulation of the program has to be used to ensure non-anticipativity of the future information. The latter refers to the fact, that at each stage only the available information at this point in time should be certain while future scenarios remain uncertain. This means that only one decision can be made at a point in time independent from the future outcomes. The result will show the optimal amounts for reinvesting maturing amounts of the replicating portfolio of fixed income securities, already taking into account the possibility of changing the reinvestment strategy at future stages.

[63] Sub-chapter 5.8 deals with the hardware restrictions on the model.

3 Modelling Main Risk Factors

The applied model framework is based on three risk factors that represent a common base in literature as presented in the previous chapter: market rates, client rates, and volumes of NMAs. This chapter explains the applied models and theories for each risk factor in detail. The trade-off between necessary sophistication and manageable implementation will have a strong influence especially on the market rate model.

Following the aim of easy realization, mathematical and statistical functions that are already incorporated in the available programs are primarily used, before doing own implementations.

An advantage of NMA models that use the three risk factors as modules in the whole framework is that each risk factor model might be changed or replaced easily. This usually doesn't require an adjustment of the whole framework or other risk factor models.

On the other hand, it is to mention that the models are dependent on each other: Especially the market rates constitute important inputs for the other two risk factors. Moreover, stochastic factors might be linked via correlations and joint distributions, which is an issue especially in the scenario generation procedure in chapter 4.2.4. These dependencies make the whole framework more complex but might be necessary to achieve results that are as close as possible to uncertain real world developments.

The above considerations require the practitioner to thoroughly check for the presence of theoretical validity of the framework every time a single risk factor model is changed.

3.1 Market Rates

Literature on term structure models seems to be vast: A wide range of models has been developed up until recent times and for most of them exist numerous papers and scientific works on their critical assessment, calibration, or empirical tests.

The most popular among them are the Vasicek[64] model (and all of its variations), the Cox-Ingersoll-Ross[65] model, the Heath-Jarrow-Morton framework[66], up to recent multifactor models[67] and the Libor-Market-Model[68].

---

[64] Vasicek (1977), pp. 177-188

One of the reasons for this strong interest in term structure models might be their application to pricing of bonds and derivatives. Having a superior model in hand, might also generate substantial economic revenue.

However, pricing of derivatives incorporates a rather short term view, and TSMs are calibrated on current market prices for that purpose, to catch the most recent market information. For a risk management purpose, which has a long-term view, a proper way to calibrate is on a time series of past data[69], to capture long term developments, particularly economic cycles.

A good TSM should be able to capture the high time variability of excess returns of government bonds over the risk-free rate as well as the time varying volatility of interest rates[70].

Empirical studies in the field of NMA valuation and risk management[71], as well as TSMs[72], provided evidence for the superiority of three-factor essentially-affine models[73].

Nevertheless, TSMs based on no-arbitrage theory have been proven to perform poorly in out-of-sample forecasting of actual interest rates[74]. For bonds and derivative pricing this might be no problem as derivatives are priced on models that use the same theoretical background. Therefore, those models are not designed to forecast the actual yield curve but rather to find a fair price of derivatives that (directly or indirectly) depend on the interest rate[75].

For the purposes of the application in a replicating portfolio the question is whether term structure models that are calculated using the unique equivalent risk measure Q are more suitable in an optimization than a model that uses real physical probabilities (probability measure P). Time-series models for past interest rates

---

[65] Cox et al. (1985), pp. 385-408

[66] Heath et al. (1992), pp. 77-105. It is actually not a model in itself, but rather a framework consistent with derivatives pricing theory to evaluate other term structure models.

[67] E.g. Dai/Singleton K.J. (2000), pp. 1943-1978, Duffee (2002), pp. 405-443

[68] E.g. Rebonato (2002), pp. 1-444

[69] Kalkbrener/Willing (2004), pp. 1549

[70] Duarte (2004), p. 379

[71] Entrop et al. (2009), pp. 1-38

[72] Huarong/Yihong (2005), 1-51

[73] As suggested by e.g. Duffee (2002), pp. 405-443

[74] Diebold/Li (2006), p. 338

[75] Laurini/Hotta (2010), p. 2.

under probability measure P[76] might provide better results in forecasting, although they lack the same theoretically sound foundation as compared to TSMs based on the Fundamental Theorem of Asset Pricing[77].

An example is the Diebold-Li model[78], which is an extension of the Nelson-Siegel Yield Curve model[79].

A drawback of those models concerning the application in this thesis is that there is no simple way shown of how to include it for example in a Monte-Carlo simulation, as they are built to produce only one best estimate. To just assume stochastic behaviour of their parameters is not a proper solution and as it is not the aim of this thesis to find eligible ways to build a stochastic extension of such an interest rate model, it is not used here. Furthermore, there is usually no arbitrage theory implicit in the model, which may lead to outcomes that clearly contradict empirical data[80].

Bardenhewer argues that interest rate risk management's focus is on the present value of an instrument and therefore the risk neutral probability measure is the correct one as opposed to liquidity risk management, which would require real world probabilities[81].

Implementing two or multifactor models as they are proposed in recent literature requires a considerable amount of resources (in the form of qualified personnel), while still having little advantage over a random walk model[82].

Following the above mentioned trade-off and the remark about easily exchangeable modules, a simple one factor Vasicek model is implemented in this thesis. Although, seemingly out of date a parsimonious model might be sufficient considering the high level of inherent uncertainty in NMAs in general[83].

---

[76] As suggested by e.g. Diebold/Li (2006), p.2

[77] Bolder (2006), p. 4

[78] Diebold/Li (2006), pp. 337-364

[79] See Nelson/Siegel (1987), pp. 473-489

[80] See Diebold/Li (2006), p. 360 (footnote), or implicitly in Bolder (2006), pp. 16-24

[81] Bardenhewer (2007), p.235.

[82] Bolder (2006), p. 75

[83] Blöchlinger (2011), p. 13

The assumptions underlying the model are:[84]

- A spot rate following a continuous Markov process.[85]
- The price of a discount bond is determined by the spot rate process over the term of the bond.
- An efficient market exists, that means no transaction costs, all information is public to all investors at the same time and investors act rational.

3.1.1 Term Structure Model

The Vasicek model can be characterized by a stochastic and mean-reverting process representing the evolution of the instantaneous interest rate (short rate):[86]

$$\mathrm{dr} = \alpha(\theta - \mathrm{r})\mathrm{dt} + \sigma\mathrm{dz}$$

The equation (also called an Ornstein-Uhlenbeck process) suggests a mean reversion, i.e. the current short rate tends towards a long term mean (θ). A larger deviation from that long term mean results in a higher probability of a movement back towards the mean. The factor α represents the speed of mean reversion. The change in the short rate (dr) in a time interval (dt) therefore is a function of: the current short rate (r), the long term mean (θ), the speed of mean reversion (α), the standard deviation of the short rate (σ) and a normally distributed random variable (dz) following a Wiener process with expectation 0 and variance dt.

As it is beyond the scope of this thesis, it is referred to Vasicek[87] for a more detailed description of the theory his model is based on.

One major drawback of this model is the assumption that rates of all maturities along the yield curve are perfectly correlated[88]. In other words, the model is basically only capable of simulating a parallel shift of the yield curve. Especially for the application in this thesis, a realistic simulation of rates with longer maturities would be useful for developing models for the client rate or NMA volumes. Perfect correlation of yields makes the use of different maturities as factors in regression functions meaningless or at least redundant.

[84] Vasicek (1977), pp. 178-179

[85] In a markov process a future value does not depend on the past history, but only on the current value. See Vasicek (1977), p. 178

[86] Vasicek (1977), p. 185

[87] Vasicek (1977), pp. 178-179

[88] Nawalkha et al. (2007), p.117

Moreover, in the short and medium term negative interest rates might occur, which empirically happened not too frequently[89].

Implementing a code, for simulating short rate paths according to the Vasicek model is a rather simple task, if the parameters of the model are known:

Given a starting value for r, only a random number from the normal distribution needs to be drawn to complete the above equation and calculate the change in the short rate for an arbitrary time increment. In R-code a matrix with different short rate paths can be generated, where each column represents one path of the interest rate and each line the new simulated rate after one month. The calculation can be done via standard algorithms using loops and matrix operations. An example code can be found in Appendix A. Figure 2 illustrates simulated paths of the short rate after calibration of the model, where the black dashed line indicates the expected value of the future rate, and the two dashed lines in blue mark the 95% confidence interval[90].

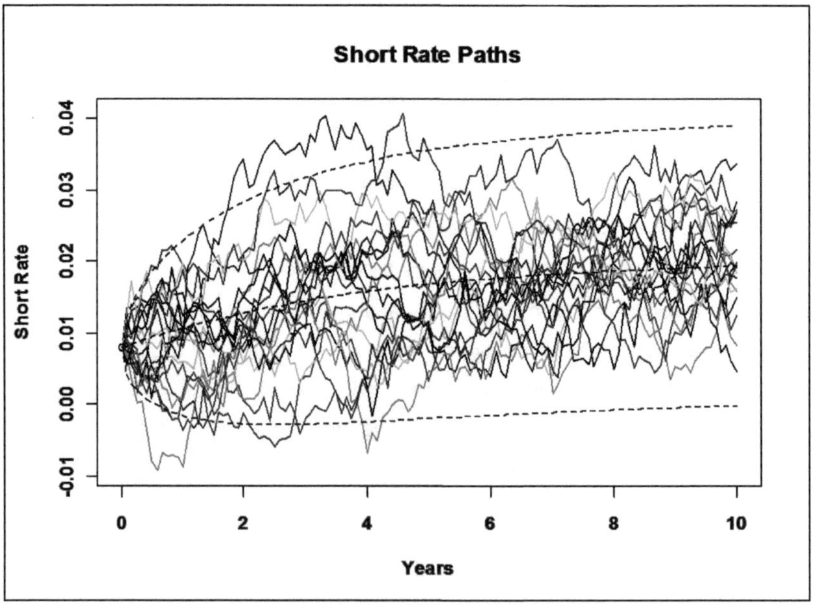

Figure 2: 20 Paths of the short rate

[89] E.g. Denmark issued T-bills "paying" negative interest on 3 and 6 month maturities on December 29th, 2011, due to troubles in the Euro zone and investors searching for safe investments.

[90] The shown paths are generated by a Monte-Carlo simulation of the stochastic factor in the model, whereas the case study will use a predefined scenario tree for this factor. See chapter 4.2.4.

The problem with negative interest rates is addressed by replacing all modelled interest rates below 1 bp by 1 bp after the calculation (in other words assuming a nominal floor at 1bp).

Given the above mentioned parameters of Vasicek's model, it is possible to calculate zero bond prices of all maturities with the following equation[91]:

$$P(t,T) = e^{A(t,T)-B(t,T)*r(t)}$$

Where

$$B(t,T) = \frac{1}{\alpha} * \{1 - e^{-\alpha*(T-t)}\},$$

$$A(t,T) = \frac{\{B(t,T) - T + t\} * \left(\alpha^2\theta - \frac{1}{2} * \sigma^2\right)}{\alpha^2} - \frac{\sigma^2 * B(t,T)^2}{4 * \alpha}$$

Having prices for all maturities available, yields can be derived by rewriting the price equation of a zero bond paying 1 in the future

$$P(t,T) = e^{-r(t)*t}$$

to

$$r(t) = -\frac{\ln\{\mathrm{P(t,T)}\}}{t}$$

This shows that in Vasicek's model, the yield curve is defined only by the three parameters (α, θ, σ).

Appendix B contains R-code for calculating a three-dimensional array, containing monthly simulated yield curve data for each path of the simulation.

As with most parametric models the calibration procedure is less simple but manageable for the one factor model and is explained after describing the data sample.

3.1.2 Data

A prerequisite for model calibration is a proper data foundation. As previously mentioned the model is calibrated on a time series of past data.

As the applied interest rate model simulates the short rate, the estimation sample consists only of representative data for the short rate. Long sample periods would be favourable, however, major changes in financial markets especially the

---

[91] Björk (2009), p. 382.

establishment of the Euro zone might have made an application of national data misleading, in particular if they lie before those changes[92].

A liquid and representative rate that has been used in previous studies is the one month Euribor (Euro Interbank Offered Rate)[93]. Additionally, these data are free and easy to collect[94]. Hence, they are used for the estimation of parameters. Monthly end of day data starting from January 1999 to December 2010 are used as estimation sample, amounting up to 144 observations.

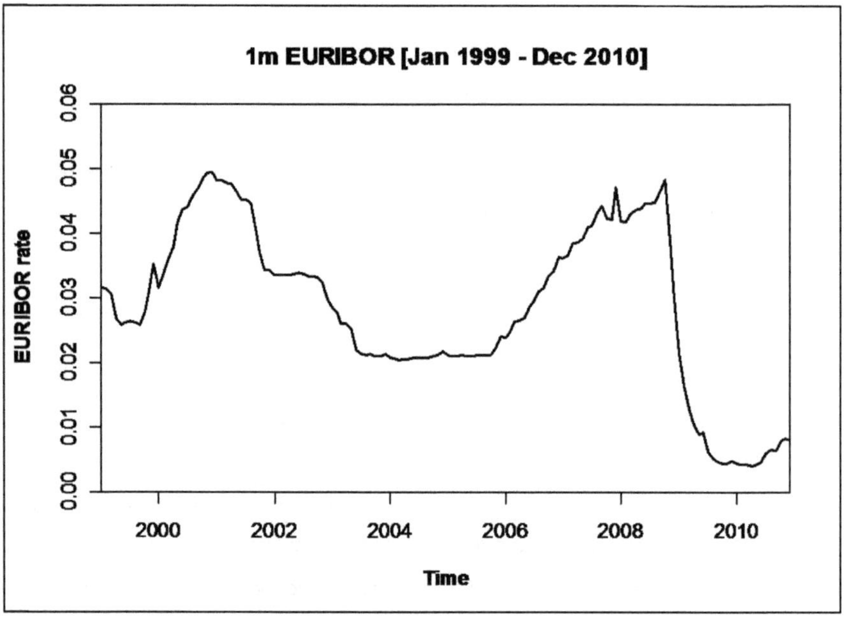

Figure 3: One month EURIBOR rate estimation sample

Figure 3 reveals some characteristics: The 1m Euribor rate increased with the two major crises, but decreased dramatically in 2009 and is still on a very low level. A mean reverting model would therefore most likely predict rising rates in the future.

---

[92] Kim/Orphanides (2005), pp. 3-4

[93] For more on Euribor see e.g.: http://www.oenb.at/de/rund_ums_geld/zinsklauseln/zinsaenderungsklauseln_vor_1.99/vibor/euribor/euribor.jsp

[94] E.g. on http://www.euribor-ebf.eu/euribor-org/euribor-rates.html or http://www.oenb.at/de/stat_melders/datenangebot/zinssaetze/eurogeldmarkt/eurogeldmarkt-_und_eurosystemzinssaetze.jsp

3.1.3 Calibration

While other interest rate models with more than one state variable (stochastic factor) are extremely difficult to estimate, a one factor Vasicek model enables the user to implement a rather straightforward likelihood function that can be solved by non-linear optimization algorithms as depicted by James and Webber[95]:

Given a time series of interest rate data r_{t_i}, where i = 1,..., N (observations), we know the transition density function for the Vasicek process is

$$p(t_{i+1}, r_{t_{i+1}}; t_i, r_{t_i} | \{\alpha, \theta, \sigma\}) = (2 * \pi * var_i)^{-\frac{1}{2}} * \exp\{-\frac{1}{2} * v^2(r_{t_i}, r_{t_{i+1}}, \Delta t_i)\}$$

where in the data used $\Delta t_i \equiv \Delta t$, meaning that all time increments are of equal length (one month) and therefore

$$var_t = \frac{\sigma^2}{2*\alpha} * (1 - e^{-2*\alpha*\Delta t}),$$

$$v(r_{t_i}, r_{t_{i+1}}, \Delta t) = \frac{r_{t_{i+1}} - (\mu + (r_{t_i} - \mu) * e^{-\alpha*\Delta t})}{\sqrt{var_t}}.$$

The likelihood function for equal time increments is

$$L = (2 * \pi * \frac{\sigma^2}{2 * \alpha} * (1 - e^{-2*\alpha*\Delta t}))^{-\frac{N-1}{2}} * \exp\{-\frac{1}{2} * v^2(r_{t_i}, r_{t_{i+1}}, \Delta t)\}$$

which gives the negative log-likelihood function

$$lnL = \frac{N-1}{2} * \ln(2 * \pi) + \frac{N-1}{2} * \ln\left(\frac{\sigma^2}{2*\alpha} * (1 - e^{-2*\alpha*\Delta t})\right) - \frac{1}{2} * \sum_{i=1}^{N-1} v^2(r_{t_i}, r_{t_{i+1}}, \Delta t).$$

Minimizing the above equation in R should be no problem, if for example the *nlm*-function (for non-linear minimization) or the *optim*-function (for general-purpose optimization including constraints) is used. However, in practice these functions might not converge to proper results, when the sample data has characteristics as the one described in the previous sub-chapter. Other, possibly more flexible and robust algorithms have been implemented in R, and are available for free on the internet.

As shown in the R-Code in Appendix C the R-function used for the minimization is the spg-function included in the BB package[96], which applies more sophisticated solution methods for non-linear objective functions.

The outcome of the calibration is shown in Table 1.

---

[95] James/Webber (2000), pp. 506-508

[96] Varadhan/Gilbert (2009)

Parameter	Starting Value	Estimated Value	Function Value	Iterations
Alpha α	0,2000	0,2367	-685,37472	2353
Theta θ	0,0284	0,0201		
Sigma σ	0,0129	0,0070		

Table 1: Parameter calibration on the sample data

As starting values for the long term mean (θ) and the standard deviation of the short rate (σ), the sample mean and standard deviation respectively are chosen. The Alpha value is a guess, however the estimation is quite stable against different starting values. The negative log-likelihood function converges, meaning a change of less than 0,00001 in the objective function after the last iteration.

3.2 Client Rates

The next step in the procedure is to set up a model for client rates[97].

Firstly, a statistical analysis of the behaviour of client rates and possibly related variables has to be carried out. This assessment shows which main characteristics the model must be able to capture.

The main features that previous studies found are[98]:

- **Client Rate Stickiness**

  This refers to the statistical fact, that client rates of most NMAs are usually stable over periods of time and changes occur only with a time lag to changes in market rates. An explanation might be that banks face administrative costs when changing rates and therefore only adjust them if the expected costs of not doing so are higher than those administrative costs[99]. Several other explanations can be found in literature, based on market concentration and market power[100], limited information of clients[101], or search and switching cost of clients[102].

  To address this property of client rates, models usually include lagged explanatory variables. Furthermore, changes in market rates of longer

[97] As mentioned above, this chronology is standard in scientific literature, but volume modeling could be regarded as a simultaneous or even preceding process.

[98] See Paraschiv/Frauendorfer (2011), pp. 3-5 for a summary of these features.

[99] Paraschiv/Frauendorfer (2011), pp. 3-4

[100] Hannan/Berger (1991), pp. 938-945.

[101] Rosen (2002), pp. 173-193.

[102] Neumark/Sharpe (1995), pp. 657-680

maturities (e.g. 5 years) have been found to influence changes in client rates to a greater extent, as they are rather stable over time[103].

- **Client Rate Jumps**
  Client rates on many NMAs are not adjusted continuously but rather occur in discrete jumps of fractions of 1 percent[104]. For NMDs, the latter might have changed since the recent financial crisis and the ongoing record low interest rate environment, in which downside corrections of fractions like 1/8 percentage points are simply not feasible from a strategic point of few[105].
  A way to incorporate this characteristic is to use an ordered logistic regression model, where a dependent variable is modelled to fit in estimated categories, which represent a certain discrete change in the client rate.
- **Asymmetric Adjustment to Market Rates**
  This refers to the different speed of adjustment to changes in market rates, when it comes to declining or increasing market rate regimes: Banks tend to adjust their client rates faster to decreases in market rates as compared to increases in market rates[106].
  An asymmetry in the speed of adjustment is captured by models that incorporate different regimes for declining or increasing rate environments. Additionally, the above mentioned ordered logistic regression is able to account for this asymmetry by estimating appropriate cut-off values for the different change categories.
- **Incomplete Adjustment to Market Rates**
  Another feature that has been found is the implicit cap in client rates, meaning that for high and still increasing market rates, the spread between market and client rates on liability side NMAs widens. That might be explained by imperfect competition and market power of banks[107].
  Incomplete adjustment could be captured in the estimation procedure of a

[103] E.g. Paraschiv/Schürle (2010), pp. 1- 28, Blöchlinger (2011), pp. 1- 47.

[104] For empirical evidence see e.g. Mester/Saunders (1995), pp. 743-764

[105] Implicit floor in client rates, competition for NMDs as "cheap" funding, etc.

[106] For empirical evidence see e.g. Neumark/Sharpe (1995), pp. 657-680 or Hannan/Berger (1991), pp. 938-945, O'Brien (2000), pp. 1-44

[107] Hutchison/Pennacchi (1996), pp. 399-417

regression function, which would result in lower coefficients for explanatory variables that indicate the level of the interest rate.

Furthermore, Kahn, Pennacchi, and Sopranzetti[108] found empirical evidence for their theory of limited customer recall abilities. They state that client rates for liability side NMAs are usually clustered at or above integers, as customers tend to remember only integer figures. To account for such a theory in a general model for interest rate pass-through is rather difficult and is not a target of the applied model in this thesis.

3.2.1 Pass-Through Model

When choosing a model it has to be taken into account that customer rates are usually only available as averages, and changes in pricing might affect only new business. This means that the jumps are not observed on an aggregate basis, but rather smoothed changes as a mixture of old and new customer rates can be observed. Next sub-chapter deals among others with this issue.

After the above considerations the task is to find a model that can deal with these characteristics. Entrop at al. conclude in their extensive empirical study, that different pass-through models make a considerable difference in their simulation approach and should therefore be of special interest for the individual bank and supervisory authorities[109].

Blöchlinger stresses the integration of the individual banks pricing strategy into a model for customer rates rather than relying on past statistics[110].

A linear regression would be easy to implement, however, it cannot properly model the asymmetry inherent in customer rates or the discrete changes[111]. While several studies reject linear regression as a suitable model, for some NMAs (mainly savings deposits) it still might produce statistically significant fits[112].

[108] Kahn et al. (1999), pp. 2185-2214

[109] Entrop et al. (2009), pp. 23-24

[110] Blöchlinger (2011), pp. 7-11

[111] Paraschiv/Frauendorfer (2011), p. 5

[112] See e.g. Entrop et al. (2009), pp. 1-38 or Janosi et al. (1999), pp. 8-31

Neumark and Sharpe developed an asymmetric pass-through model that basically extends the regression model by introducing two different regimes that are triggered by an indicator function[113].

A quite promising class of models are (threshold) error-correction models, which have been implemented in an NMA context by Paraschiv and Schürle[114] and Paraschiv and Frauendorfer[115] respectively. These models incorporate an equilibrium relationship (defined by a cointegration vector) between market and customer rates and provide fairly well fits and good out-of-sample performance[116].

However, in this thesis a multinomial ordered logistic regression approach is applied, which models the change in the customer rate. The general model is now specified[117]:

We define a latent control variable z_i^* that is sorted into a set of possible discrete changes in the interest rate categories 0,1,..., J for time steps *i*:

$$z_i^* = \alpha' w_i + u_i;$$

$$z_i = \begin{cases} 0\ if -\infty < z_i^* \leq \mu_1, \\ 1\ if\ \mu_1 < z_i^* \leq \mu_2, \\ 2\ if\ \mu_2 < z_i^* \leq \mu_3, \\ \vdots \\ J\ if\ \mu_J < z_i^* < \infty \end{cases}$$

where α is a vector of coefficients to be estimated, u_i is a standard normal (probit model) or log-normally (logit model) distributed error term. The ordered cutoff values $\mu_1 < \mu_2 < \cdots < \mu_J$ have to be estimated simultaneously with the coefficients. $\mu_0 \equiv -\infty$ and $\mu_{J+1} \equiv \infty$ are the outer cutoffs. Vector w_i contains observations of certain explanatory variables and the change categories are as well observed from time-series data of customer rates. The latent variable z_i^* on the other hand cannot be observed.

The client rate c_i therefore is defined as $c_i = c_{i-1} + z_i$ (change in customer rate).

---

[113] O'Brien (2000), pp. 3-4, originally developed by Neumark/Sharpe (1992).

[114] Paraschiv/Schürle (2010), pp. 1-24

[115] Paraschiv/Frauendorfer (2011), pp. 1-56

[116] Paraschiv/Frauendorfer (2011), pp. 13-24

[117] According to the representation in Chiburis/Lokshin (2007), p. 168

Frauendorfer and Schürle apply this model by using the lagged customer rate and current and past values of the "level" factor of their two factor Vasicek TSM as explanatory variables[118].

Blöchlinger uses a short term rate, and spreads between (lagged) customer rates and short/long term market rates in the regression function for the latent control variable[119].

A main assumption behind this model is the above mentioned distribution of the error term u_i of the control variable, as it cannot be observed empirically.

The model is chosen because it features discrete changes (via categories), asymmetric adjustment (via thresholds), rate stickiness (via lagged parameters), and possible incomplete adjustment (via regression parameters). A drawback might be that it doesn't consider any long-term equilibrium between client and market rates and deviations thereof.

Furthermore strategic policies for client rates can be integrated in the model.

An implicit floor, $\overline{c_l}$, and/or cap, $\overline{c_h}$, in client rates is incorporated by extending the client rate function to[120]:

$$c_i = \min\{\max\{c_{i-1} + z_i, \overline{c_l}\}, \overline{c_h}\}.$$

To implement a forward looking model, Blöchlinger[121] suggests adjusting the estimated coefficients to match a possible new strategy[122]. Additionally, he proposes adding a volume term to the regression equation, to account for the influence of aggregated volumes on pricing behaviour[123].

In this case study, both suggested regression formulas are applied and estimated. Moreover, the same floor as for the market rate (1 bp) is applied. An example R-Code for the client rate can be found in Appendix D.

---

118 Frauendorfer/Schürle (2007), pp. 345-346

119 Blöchlinger (2011), pp. 9-11

120 Blöchlinger (2011), pp. 9-10

121 Blöchlinger (2011), p. 10

122 E.g. if the bank decides to apply a more competitive pricing strategy with lower anticipated spreads, the coefficient of the spread variable can be manually increased to account for that change.

123 Blöchlinger (2011), p. 11

3.2.2 Data

As mentioned above, current and past short and long term market rates, past client rates, spreads between those rates and a wide variety of alternative measures[124] might serve as data inputs for the model. For future simulations values for market rates are derived from the TSM described in sub-chapter 3.1. Possible deficiencies of the TSM are therefore handed over to the client rate model.

In particular, one month Euribor data are used for the short-term rate, and five year Euro-Swaps[125] data represent a long-term market rate. Client rate and volume data as well as possible other customer specific explanatory variables have to be taken from internal databases.

In this thesis we calibrate the client rate and volume model on a data sample of aggregated retail savings accounts from a Euro zone bank.

The main data issue for this model is that it requires a certain sample size to be properly estimated. This can be a problem with customer rate data of new products and too small time series due to infrequent data points (e.g. monthly).

Moreover, the issue that discrete jumps in the client rate are usually not observed on an aggregate basis has to be addressed[126]. To be able to calibrate the model past changes have to be mapped to change categories to create a suitable time series. A simple mapping procedure is integrated in the R-Code for the Calibration in Appendix D, where every change in client rate is rounded to the closest twentieth of a percentage point[127].

3.2.3 Calibration

The calibration of an ordered logistic regression is usually done by a maximum likelihood procedure. Conditional probabilities for the control variable to be below a certain threshold are defined. A proper maximum likelihood procedure must take the correct order of the thresholds into account. In R the function polr() is already

---

[124] E.g. NMA volumes or customer data, like gender, age, etc.

[125] These should be available in any bank's risk management system, as swaps are the standard instrument for hedging interest rate risk. However, the data for this thesis are extracted directly from a commercial data provider and represent ask-quotations of Euro-Swap rates.

[126] See 3.2.1 for an explanation.

[127] A similar approach is chosen by Paraschiv/Frauendorfer (2011), p. 28

implemented as part of the MASS[128] package for this purpose. However, to be able to use this function the data has to be provided in the correct way.

All the above mentioned data is firstly loaded into R, then manipulated as required and finally merged to one data frame object for easy use in the calibration function. Appendix E contains the applied R-Code for the calibration procedure explaining each step of the procedure.

The data samples available for NMDs in this thesis consist of 30 monthly observations of client rates. However, there are only very few observations of client rate changes different to zero, providing zero or only one observation for some client rate change categories. This is also caused by the very low interest rate environment in the Euro zone, throughout the sample period beginning at January 2009 and lasting until June 2011. Subsequent data (until May 2012) is used for out of sample testing.

Unfortunately, this leads to rather poor, statistically not very significant outcomes. The tables below show outputs of different model specifications. Table 2 (a) and (b) show the regression outcomes using the above described formulas by Blöchlinger[129] and Frauendorfer and Schürle[130], respectively. They yield a very poor fit for both the regression parameters and the threshold intercepts judging by their t-statistics (mostly below the rule of thumb (absolute) value of two, meaning insignificant results).

Coefficients			
Variable	Value	Std.Error	t-value
Short Term Rate	-433,935	229,286	-1,893
Spread (Short Term)	-600,534	246,975	-2,432
Spread (Long Term)	-672,216	150,496	-0,447

Thresholds			
Categories	Value	Std.Error	t-value
-0,004|-0,0015	-6,438	3,747	-1,718
-0,0015|-0,001	-5,401	3,552	-1,520
-0,001|-5e-04	-4,131	3,443	-1,200
-5e-04|0	-3,320	3,394	-0,978
0|0,002	1,162	3,504	0,332
0,002|0,0025	1,866	3,578	0,522

(a)

Coefficients			
Variable	Value	Std.Error	t-value
Client Rate (Lag)	-696,184	260,985	-2,668
Short Term Rate	-42,995	252,788	-0,170
Short Term Rate (Lag)	189,344	255,166	0,742

Thresholds			
Categories	Value	Std.Error	t-value
-0,004|-0,0015	-5,694	3,602	-1,581
-0,0015|-0,001	-4,696	3,442	-1,364
-0,001|-5e-04	-3,479	3,350	-1,039
-5e-04|0	-2,710	3,305	-0,820
0|0,002	1,577	3,435	0,459
0,002|0,0025	2,282	3,510	0,650

(b)

Table 2: Regression outcomes for Blöchlinger's (a) and Frauendorfer/Schürle's (b) formula.

[128] Venables/Ripley (2002)

[129] Blöchlinger (2011), pp. 9-11

[130] Frauendorfer/Schürle (2007), pp. 345-346

In Table 3 a different specification is chosen:

Coefficients			
Variable	Value	Std.Error	t-value
Short Term Rate (Lag)	-619,392	2,374	-2,609
Spread (Short Term)	-790,788	2,730	-2,897

Thresholds			
Categories	Value	Std.Error	t-value
-0,004|-0,0015	-9,284	2,776	-3,345
-0,0015|-0,001	-8,101	2,354	-3,441
-0,001|-5e-04	-6,754	2,156	-3,132
-5e-04|0	-5,914	2,060	-2,871
0|0,002	-1,426	1,704	-0,837
0,002|0,0025	-0,725	1,848	-0,392

Table 3: Regression outcome applied model

- To account for the deficiencies of the term structure model in forecasting realistic long term rates, only short term variables are used.
- The remaining possible variables are chosen by stepwise regression (forward selection and backward elimination) using t-statistics.

The final regression function makes use of the lagged (one month) short term rate and the lagged spread to the short term rate (last client rate minus last short term rate).

The negative coefficients for the parameters of the regression formula are in line with Blöchlinger's result[131], who explains the negative value for the short term rate coefficient by an implicit rate cap on the client rate. The negative coefficient for the spread is quite intuitive yielding a higher probability of client rate increases when the (absolute) spread gets wider, and thus a higher probability of narrowing the gap again.

The coefficients in the regression function and most of the thresholds are significant judging by their t-statistics, whereas the thresholds for positive changes in client rates have quite low t-values. The latter is due to a lack of sufficient observations for the categories.

Although the model performs best in in-sample tests as compared to other model specifications the results show only moderate accuracy as depicted in Figure 4. Here we can clearly observe the models difficulty in dealing with the (infrequent and high) positive change observations. However, the model provides at least plausible changes in both directions, when applied in the simulation framework.

[131] Blöchlinger (2011), p. 37

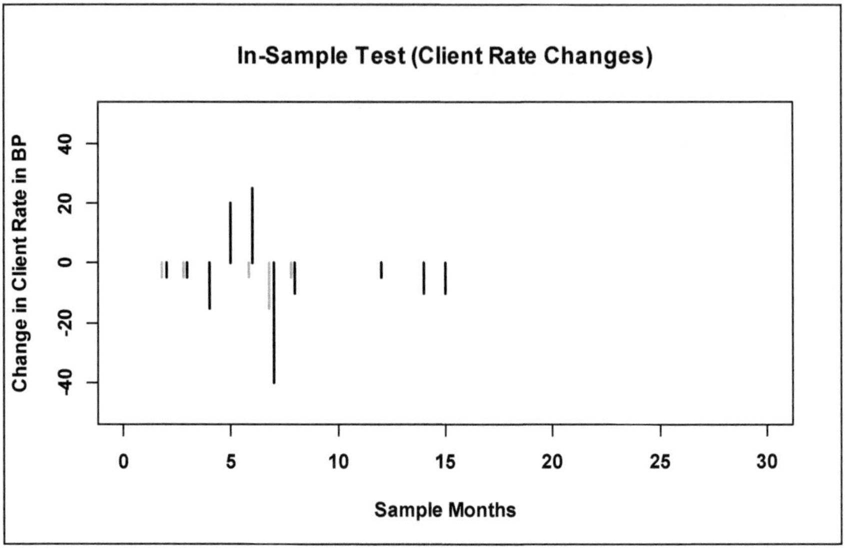

Figure 4: Client rate model in-sample test with empirical data (black) and model output (grey)

3.3 Total Volumes of Non-Maturing Accounts

The first question that has to be answered is which of the following cases is intended to be modelled: Total volumes of NMAs or retained NMA balances. Data for the latter is hard to get, causing scientific literature to focus rather on total NMA volume evolution. In some studies[132], the volume is just assumed to be constant or decreasing by an arbitrary rate.

The outflow pattern of retained balances might also be added exogenously as constraints in the optimization procedure in the form of upper bounds for the respective time buckets.

If the model would be intended to value the NMA position the following decision criteria would be relevant[133]:

The viewpoint of an investor is rather concerned with total volume evolution, to include expected future profits, whereas a regulator wants to examine the potential cost in the course of a bankruptcy and therefore analyse retained balances.

[132] E.g. Entrop et al. (2009), pp. 1-38

[133] Sheehan (2004), p. 9

However, an empirical analysis on retained balances shows that expected lives of deposits are generally much higher, than those suggested by regulators. Yet calculating retained balances from data of times of normal business activity (before a possible bankruptcy) might not be a proper methodology considering the goal of a regulator. An internal use of data reported to regulators might, however, in the case of NMAs lead to wrong business decisions.

More relevant for this thesis is the question if there should be made a difference for internal use of a model for either liquidity or interest rate risk management[134]:

In a replicating portfolio approach, as it is used in this thesis, total volumes can be modelled, while liquidity risks can be considered in the restrictions on the optimization model of the replicating portfolio.

Volume evolutions of NMAs might be quite different depending on the product type. However, scientific literature and empirical studies mainly focus on non-maturing deposit (NMD) volumes[135]. Also the implementations in this thesis rather correspond to NMDs. Nevertheless, the same models might be used for other NMA products by searching for the most suitable explanatory variables of this specific product.

Empirical findings[136] using Swiss national bank data say that when market interest rates rise, the total balance of NMA falls, as customers try take advantage of the higher interest rates by investing their cash in other products, like bonds[137].

Furthermore, if interest rates are low, the spread between an alternative investment and client rates becomes narrow, and therefore NMD volumes are large. This suggests that deposit volumes depend on the level of interest rates.

However, other studies haven't found such a clear correlation[138].

Additionally, the slope of the yield curve can be an explanatory variable, especially with term deposits[139].

---

[134] Bardenhewer (2007), pp. 227-229.

[135] Which makes sense given that they represent by far the largest share of total NMA volumes in a bank.

[136] See e.g. Frauendorfer/Schürle (2007), or Paraschiv/Frauendorfer (2011)

[137] Cipu/Udriste (2009), p. 369

[138] Kalkbrener/Willing (2004), p. 1549

[139] Paraschiv/Frauendorfer (2011), p.34

Client rates affect volumes of NMAs, as they pose a bank individual factor that can be administered deliberately[140]. Clients should primarily deposit money with or borrow money from the bank that offers the best rates from their point of view. This reasoning should be valid for any kind of NMA.

Furthermore, previous volumes clearly have an influence on the current volume. This can be incorporated by adding the lagged volume as explanatory variable into a regression function[141] or by formulating an autoregressive model[142].

Moreover, macro-economic variables, like GDP, financial indices, unemployment rates, etc. may influence the volumes of NMAs. However, they are usually not included in volume models in practise[143], as forecasting them is barely possible[144] and can therefore not be used in forward looking simulation models.

To account for the uncertainties in a model that knowingly excludes possible variables with high explanatory power, some volume model approaches include an additional stochastic factor[145].

Finally, seasonality patterns might be found in time series of NMA volumes, which in the case of NMDs might be explained by regional payment patterns of remunerations, holiday expenditures, or others. In a regression function, such patterns could be captured by adding dummy variables for the respective months or quarters[146].

3.3.1 Volume Model

An intuitive and simple way to capture the above information in a model is a simple regression formula, though empirical studies[147] found the residuals of the regression to be serially correlated. In such a case, the ordinary regression model has to be extended to account for autoregression in errors.

[140] Paraschiv/Frauendorfer (2011), pp. 33-34

[141] As in Frauendorfer/Schürle (2007), p. 347

[142] As in Paraschiv/Schürle (2010), pp. 19-20

[143] One exception is O'Brien (2000), pp. 8-9. He includes local income levels as explanatory variables in his model. However, he didn't find them to be significant in his empirical study.

[144] Kalkbrener/Willing (2004), p. 1566

[145] See e.g. Kalkbrener/Willing (2004), pp. 1557-1558, or Frauendorfer/Schürle (2007), p. 347

[146] See Bardenhewer (2007), p.239, or Paraschiv/Frauendorfer (2011), p. 37.

[147] See e.g. Paraschiv/Schürle (2010), pp. 19-20.

The model applied in this thesis is based on the model of Paraschiv and Frauendorfer[148] with the difference that logarithmic volume changes are used as dependent variable instead of the plain volume change:

$$ln\Delta V_t = \beta_0 + \beta x_t + \alpha_t + \varepsilon_t$$

$$\varepsilon_t = AR(i)_{\epsilon_{t-i}} + u_t$$

Where the logarithmic change in NMA volume ($ln\Delta V_t$) is a function of a vector of explanatory variables (x_t) and their coefficients (β), seasonal dummy variables (α_t) and an error term (ε_t). The latter is expected to be autocorrelated and therefore its function includes autoregressive terms ($AR(i)_{\epsilon_{t-i}}$), where i stands for the order of autoregression.

Furthermore, the case study in this thesis follows the above mentioned approach to include an additional stochastic factor that is uncorrelated with the one from the Vasicek model. This is how the uncertainty (represented by the residuals) in volumes is accounted for, which is not covered by the regression model. The mean of this factor therefore is zero, as we assume the error term to be and its standard deviation equals the one from the regression residuals.

The fact that the volume model exhibits no mean reversion might cause a need for upper and especially for lower limits to keep scenarios in a reasonable range. Usually the scenarios of the stochastic factor in the volume model also include a decline scenario. This decline scenario is followed by another decline scenario in the next stage and so on. Although the probability of such harsh cumulated decline scenarios in higher stages gets negligibly small, they significantly influence the minimum weights constraint in the MSP as is described in the chapter 5.2.3.2. Moreover, it might be unreasonable from an economic perspective to assume them in the first place.

One way to limit drastic declines or increases in volume throughout the simulation period is to look at past declines/increases over certain time periods. The following procedure is implemented in the volume scenario generation procedure:

- Firstly, the maximum volume decline/increase in the past over stepwise (one month) increasing time periods from one month to the maximum length of the simulation period is calculated.

[148] Paraschiv/ Frauendorfer (2011), p. 37

- Secondly, these maximum declines and increases are adjusted with a multiplier to form lower and upper limits for the respective period. The multiplier is an external input that reflects the individual risk aversion.
- Thirdly, the generated volume scenarios are checked for limit excesses, which are then set back to the maximum allowed limit.

Finally, it should be noted that models that include behavioural elements appropriately might be even more suitable in practical applications[149].

3.3.2 Data

As data for the estimation of the model we take the same long and short term rates as in the risk factor models, as well as client rates, spreads, and NMD volumes from the above described data sample. Possible seasonal patterns are captured by monthly dummy variables. The calibration procedure includes R-code for the generation of the latter. Furthermore, simulated market and client rates are used as input factors in the forecasting function.

3.3.3 Calibration

In a first step an appropriate regression function has to be found. This is done in this thesis by backward selecting of explanatory variables according to their significance after ordinary least squares (OLS) estimation, seeking a maximum explanatory power of the model (measured by the coefficient of determination R^2).

This linear model can be calibrated by using the lm-function, which is included in the standard version of R and performs the required OLS estimation.

After calibrating the regression formula the residuals have to be checked for autocorrelation. The ar-formula can be used for that purpose: This formula can deliver the best fit autocorrelation order according to the Akaike information criterion (AIC)[150]. The results of this formula, namely the order and coefficients of autocorrelation, can be used directly for the next calculations.

Indeed, the residuals from the OLS exhibit autocorrelation with the data samples used for this thesis. Only lag orders of one are found to be the best fit for the residuals. The general reason for autocorrelated residuals in linear regression models that might apply in this case is the non-consideration of at least one key

[149] Such an approach by Nyström (2008) is outlined in sub-chapter 2.2.

[150] Akaike (1974), pp. 716-723

predictor variable[151]. This might be the for example the deliberately omitted macro-economic factors.

However, if such variables are not available, one way to fix this problem is by performing a Cochrane-Orcutt procedure[152]:

Starting from the original linear model of the form described above, and the coefficients φ_j where j = 1, 2, ...,n (order of integration) of the estimated autocorrelation in residuals, we transform the time series of dependent and independent variables so that

$$ln\Delta V_t^* = ln\Delta V_t - \varphi_1 * ln\Delta V_{t-1} - \cdots - \varphi_n * ln\Delta V_{t-n}$$

$$x_t^* = x_t - \varphi_1 * x_{t-1} - \cdots - \varphi_n * x_{t-n}$$

The transformed time series are now used again in a linear model

$$ln\Delta V_t^* = \beta_0^* + \beta^* x_t^* + \alpha_t + \varepsilon_t$$

and the OLS estimation is performed. If the residuals are still autocorrelated afterwards, the procedure is repeated with the newly estimated coefficients φ_j. If the autocorrelation was successfully removed, the regression parameters for the original model are obtained by taking

$$\beta = \beta^*$$

$$\beta_0 = \frac{\beta_0^*}{1 - \varphi_1 - \cdots - \varphi_n}$$

To make forecasting theoretically sound the above described correlation in error terms should be taken into account[153]. Since a stochastic term is included, which represents the forecasting error in the simulation, also the autocorrelation between these error terms has to be considered.

Appendix G and H contain R-Code for an OLS regression as well as for the Cochrane-Orcutt procedure. The simulation procedure for the volume model written in R can be found in Appendix F.

---

[151] Kutner et al. (2005), p. 490

[152] The specific methodology is based on Kutner et al. (2005), p. 490-495 and Cochrane/Orcutt (1949), pp.32-61.

[153] Kutner et al. (2005), pp. 499-500

The output of the (first) regression as depicted in Table 4 shows the following outcome:

- The applied model after using stepwise regression includes the same variables as for the client rate model (lagged short term market rate and spread between the latter and the client rate). Additionally it found dummy variables for June and July to be significant, which might be explained by local remuneration laws and holiday specific behaviour.
- The significance levels for the coefficients are satisfactory for the purposes of the thesis (assuming a minimum confidence level of 95%).
- The residual standard error of 4,8% of the total NMA volume is acceptable and will be used as standard deviation of the stochastic factor in the volume simulation model. As absolute amounts are modelled, the relative change is multiplied by the NMA volume of the previous period.
- The adjusted R-Squared shows an explanatory power of the model of about 32% of the actual development. Combined with a stochastic factor the model should provide us with sufficiently reasonable forecasts.
- The maximum residual might be used as an absolute lower limit for short term investments in the optimization procedure for the replicating portfolio, if no other liquidity restrictions apply.

Regression Output and Analysis					
	Estimate	Std. Error	t-value	Pr(>|t|)	Sig.Code
(Intercept)	-0,11	0,04	-2,52	0,02	*
Short Term rate (Lag)	13,96	5,48	2,55	0,02	*
Spread (Short Term)	14,98	5,78	2,59	0,02	*
June (Dummy)	0,10	0,04	2,67	0,01	*
July (Dummy)	0,10	0,04	2,28	0,03	*

Signif.code:	< 0,05 '*'				
Residual Standard Error:		0,05729	on 24 Degrees of Freedom		
Multiple R-Squared		0,4183	Adjusted R-Squared		0,3214

Residuals:	
Min.	-0,119
1Q	-0,032
Median	0,004
3Q	0,021
Max	0,150

Table 4: OLS regression output of the volume model calibration

However, the residuals are autocorrelated by order one with coefficient 0,379, which is used to adjust the regression coefficients according to the above explained Cochrane-Orcutt procedure (results in Table 5) and also for the error terms in forecasting.

Coefficients After Cochrane-Orcutt Procedure						
	(Intercept)	Short Term Rate (Lag)	Spread (Short Term)	January	June	July
Estimate	-14,785	2.166,348	1.817,894	-23,817	14,100	13,418

Table 5: Regression coefficients after Cochrane-Orcutt procedure

The resulting model shows satisfying results in an in-sample test (Figure 5).

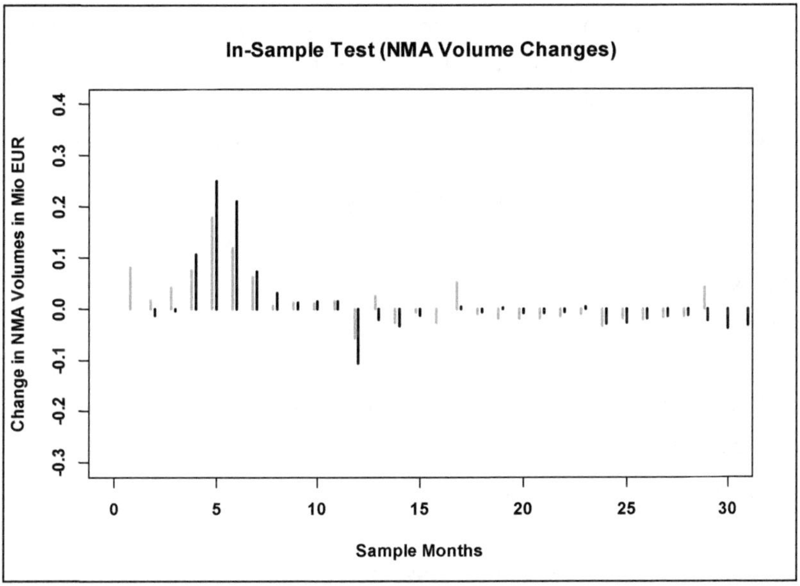

Figure 5: NMA volume model in-sample test with empirical data (black) and model output (grey)

4 Setting up a Multistage Stochastic Program

Having proper risk factor models implemented, the next step is to develop a replicating portfolio methodology that defines the objective function and the constraints of the optimization procedure. Once this is done, a scenario tree will be generated, which predefines the stochastic factors of the risk factor models. Subsequently, future paths of the risk factors can be easily calculated, taking the stochastic factors from the scenario tree as input. To make the whole model framework computationally tractable, a certain complexity reduction technique will be applied to the MSP or more precisely to the scenario generation procedure.

4.1 Replicating Portfolio Methodology

The aim of a replicating portfolio in the NMA context is straightforward: Represent complex NMAs with a portfolio of plain vanilla (zero) bonds to make NMAs manageable.

However, there is no single right way to do this and several models have been depicted in scientific literature, which differ among other details in the following main characteristics:

- **Set of investable products**
  Yields taken for the respective maturities might be derived in different ways or from different products, as zero curves themselves are usually not directly observable in total.
  Moreover, the granularity of different maturities and the length of the longest investable term differ among approaches in literature.
- **Short sales**
  Short sales are explicitly not allowed in the larger part of models suggested in literature. However, Blöchlinger points out, that the option like payoff of NMAs cannot possibly be represented by plain vanilla bonds without allowing for short sales[154]. Also the preceding studies[155] on dynamic modelling via an MSP tolerate short sales, when it is necessary for liquidity purposes.

[154] Blöchlinger (2011), p. 20

[155] See e.g. Frauendorfer/Schürle (2007), p. 354.

- **Length of time horizon**

  The choice of the time horizon on which the replicating portfolio is optimized and therefore for hedging decisions is an important input factor[156] and ranges from eight[157] up to 30[158] years in scientific literature (static models). Furthermore, it is suggested that this period covers at least one economic cycle[159]. However, for simulation approaches it might be difficult to implement longer term models. Firstly, the simulation of longer periods adds a lot uncertainty and increases model risk. Secondly, a longer time horizon creates problems with tractability, particularly with multistage stochastic programming. The latter problem limits the feasible planning horizon considerably on an ordinary work station. Frauendorfer and Schürle[160] implement a seven years simulation period by allowing for yearly changes (as opposed to monthly in this case study) in the reinvestment policy.

- **Investment Policy (Initial Application)**

  The model might be specified so that the absolute amount invested in one maturity is done by one single transaction at one point in time[161], or it is assumed to be evenly distributed between the current date and all points in time until maturity[162]. The difference is not only in the cash flow pattern (smaller portions of principles are repaid frequently versus one large amount is repaid at maturity), but also in yields (yield to maturity of one product vs. an average of possibly more products).

- **Yields of the Initial Portfolio**

  If one choses the even distribution of amounts, which is the usual approach in literature, it is not straightforward to obtain the respective yields. For example investing in a 60 month contract with three months maturity generally wouldn't be possible at the nominal (par) value due to changes in the yield curve since its issuance among other things. This problem in the beginning is circumvented by sticking to the rule of how absolute amounts

---

[156] Blöchlinger (2011), p. 20

[157] See Blöchlinger (2011), p. 39

[158] E.g. O'Brien (2000), p.15 or Office of Thrift Supervision (2001)

[159] Bardenhewer (2007), p. 230

[160] Frauendorfer/Schürle (2007), p. 352.

[161] See e.g. Maes/Timmermans (2005), pp. 146-147

[162] See e.g. Bardenhewer (2007), p. 226

for each contract are calculated, but investing only in newly issued instruments at the beginning. That means that e.g. the amount calculated for a three month MMD with two months until maturity is initially invested in a newly issued MMD with two months maturity. If such a product is not available, an existing product with the desired time to maturity can be considered with its current market price and yield. When this product matures the amounts can be reinvested in the "real" three month MMD.

- **Frequency of recalculation**
  On the one hand, models might be recalculated on a regular basis (monthly, quarterly, semi-annually, or yearly), where the risk of bigger changes in the composition of the portfolio increases with longer time horizons[163]. On the other hand, recalculation could be triggered by significant changes in the relevant environment and variables[164] (e.g. market rate movements, NMA volume changes, etc.).
- **Liquidity Restrictions**
  Models might include special restrictions or requirements to account for the liquidity risk inherent in NMAs. Restrictions might take the form of absolute or relative, upper or lower limits invested in different time buckets.
- **Treatment of significant portfolio changes**
  Should the weights change drastically after an optimization procedure, it might be necessary that positions are (fictitiously) closed and invested in other maturities. The model might differ in how the losses or gains[165] from these transactions are treated and which department in the bank should bear a loss[166]. Blöchlinger further suggests distributing the gain or loss over time and including it that way in FTP calculations[167]. Practically, it is rather omitted in FTP calculations and regarded as a model deficiency.
- **Share of total NMA volume to be modelled**
  Maes and Timmermans suggest not to use the entire NMA amount in the

---

[163] See e.g. Maes/Timmermans (2005) or Bardenhewer (2007)

[164] This idea is brought forward by Blöchlinger (2011), pp. 21-22

[165] These losses or gains do not actually occur, as the replicating portfolio is a theoretical construct. However, all of the gains and losses associated with it should be included in an FTP calculation.

[166] Frauendorfer/Schürle (2007), p. 332

[167] Blöchlinger (2011), p. 22

optimization procedure, but rather to divide them in a first step into core deposits (invested in a long horizon), volatile deposits (invested in the shortest time bucket), and the remainder (actually used in the optimization procedure)[168].

Moreover, all models in literature agree in the goal of keeping (theoretical) transaction costs low, therefore pursuing a buy-and-hold strategy for every product acquired as long as it is (theoretically) feasible.

Next to advantages such as manageability and tangibility Dewachter, Lyrio, and Maes describe the following major drawbacks of a replicating portfolio approach[169]:

- These models are inconsistent with the no-arbitrage principle, which is currently an integrated part in most asset pricing methodologies.
- There is no possibility to derive an economic value of NMAs.
- Model outputs vary significantly if a different optimization objective is chosen or a different set of investable assets is applied.

The internal inconsistency with the no-arbitrage principle could be solved by simulating market rates under probability measure P, which is not attempted in this thesis.

Not being able to determine a specific NPV of NMAs for the bank is not a problem as long as they can still be properly hedged. If accounting rules for banks would be changed, so that it is possible to account for fair values of assets and liabilities, a calculation of an NPV for NMAs would be necessary. However, the banking market developments and events in recent years rather have increased public distrust towards banks and therefore a change in accounting rules is highly unlikely in the near future.

The third model disadvantage is hard to overcome. In practise the strategically most suitable objective criterion should be chosen by the bank. Moreover, a realistic set of investable assets should be specified, focusing on liquidity in the respective market. When it comes to the choice of maturities, individual banks might choose different maximum maturities according to their level of risk aversion and lower granularity for simplicity of implementation.

[168] Maes/Timmermans (2005), p. 146

[169] Dewachter et al. (2006), p. 21

However, the possibility of influencing the replicating portfolio structure and thus also FTP prices by choosing different objective criteria could make the model vulnerable for agency problems as it might have a huge impact on the results of profit centers that depend on FTP.

4.1.1 Optimization and Investment Policy

The principle of the optimization is as follows: Given known relative costs of the NMA (client rate plus relative servicing costs plus a margin), fit amounts of reinvestments of maturing tranches (plus/minus a volume change) in specified products with known yields so that over an arbitrary period of time a certain objective criterion is met. This criterion can be for example the minimization of the standard deviation of the spread between NMA costs and replicating portfolio yield[170], the maximization of the Sharpe ratio[171] of this spread[172], the minimization of the expected downside risk of not meeting NMA costs[173], maximizing the expected NPV of the replicating portfolio return[174], etc. However, for the application in an MSP linear objective criteria are preferred, so that efficient and reliable solving algorithms, like the Simplex[175] algorithm, can be applied. When doing this optimization several restrictions must be met to ensure compliance with the investment policy defined for the replicating portfolio. Their mathematical definition is shown in subchapter 4.2.1.

Based on Bardenhewer's replicating portfolio the investment policy in this thesis has the following specifications[176]:

- The set of investable securities is defined by:
  Maturity buckets of one, three, and six months as well as five years. For a comparison the model is also applied using additional securities of one, two, three, and four years.
  Money market product prices like MMDs are used as benchmark for

---

170 See e.g. Maes/Timmermans (2005), p. 146, or Blöchlinger (2011), p. 21.

171 This refers to the "reward-to-variability-ratio" (risk-adjusted return measure) named after and first mentioned in Sharpe (1966). It is calculated by dividing the return by its standard deviation over a period.

172 Maes/Timmermans (2005), p. 145

173 Frauendorfer/Schürle (2007), p. 339

174 Forrest et al. (1997), p. 384

175 Dantzig (1963), pp. 94-110

176 Bardenhewer (2007), pp. 225-230

maturities up to one year (EURIBOR rates), and Euro swap quotations for longer maturities.

- The nominal[177] volume of the replicating portfolio must at all times equal the volume of the NMA modelled.
- Every product type with maturity *j* (in months) consists of *j* possible contracts with differing times to maturity ranging from one to *j* months. For example the three months MMD consists of three contracts with times to maturity of one, two, and three months.
- The initial absolute amount invested in a product is uniformly distributed among all those contracts. This indicates that every month a jth of the total initial amount invested in a product matures and can be reinvested with the same or possibly new weights (now assuming a constant NMA volume). As mentioned above, to be theoretically sound, this would require a lot of different products and their yields, when e.g. the amount for the 60 month time bucket is evenly distributed to each month from one to 60. For the case study a simpler approach is applied, which assumes that all those amounts had already been invested at the time of issuance of the respective product. This allows for using only current and historical rates of the investable securities. In practical terms, this assumes that the replicating portfolio had been in place for 60 months already. Or one simply regards the returns of the portfolio as not accurate as long as products from the initial portfolio are part of the replicating portfolio (in this case 60 months at maximum). As the static model uses the same methodology to calculate yields comparability is still provided.
- The amounts invested in the one month maturity bucket must at all times cover the relative maximum outflow in the past, times an individual multiplier[178], which is set to two in the case study. This serves as a liquidity buffer and provides a lower absolute limit.

Additional liquidity risk restrictions as the "Market Mix" portfolio by Bardenhewer[179] or buffer functions of the one month bucket should not be needed in a dynamic

---

[177] Market values should not be necessary, if the model strictly pursues a buy-and-hold strategy.

[178] This external input should reflect the individual (liquidity) risk aversion level.

[179] Bardenhewer (2007), pp. 231-232

model that can adjust weights over time, is frequently recalculated, and incorporates numerous decline scenarios.

The above described policies with a few liquidity related extensions can be used as a static model as well and serve as such as a benchmark for the dynamic model in subchapter 5.2. Additionally, the static model can be used to create an "initial portfolio", which can be seen as a starting point, when the dynamic model is first applied.

4.1.2 Yields and Data

For the case study data should contain zero curve yields of different maturities relevant for European Union based banking groups. As par-bond prices and yields are publicly available on a daily basis usually without costs, they could be used to calculate a zero curve[180]. However, these yields need to be actually investable and therefore be based on a liquid market. For that purpose money market yields are used for maturities up to one year and swap rates for longer maturities. These yields might be extracted from commercial data providers, or in some form from the ECB, or other webpages. This thesis makes use of Euribor rates representing MMDs and Euro Swap rates (extracted from a Bloomberg system) for longer term rates.

4.2 Optimization Problem

The optimization problem is formulated and "solved as a large scale linear or quadratic program"[181]. The general form of a linear program exhibits the following form[182]:

$$\left.\begin{array}{rr} & min\ c^T x \\ \text{subject to} & Ax \propto b \\ & l \leq x \leq u \end{array}\right\},$$

Where x is a vector of decision variables to be found, $c \in \mathbb{R}^n$ and $b \in \mathbb{R}^m$ are vectors of known coefficients, and $A \in \mathbb{R}^{n \times m}$ is a matrix of known coefficients. l and u represent lower and upper bounds of x. The bound l is usually assumed to be zero while u is theoretically infinity, but can in practise be approximated by a sufficiently large number. In the case study, variables for the deviation from an

[180] E.g. Svensson (1994)

[181] Zanjani et al. (2009), p. 4702

[182] Kall/Mayer (2010), p. 1

NMA cost plus a margin will used, therefore relaxing the standard assumption and allowing for negative values for these variables.

Moreover, practical applications might require that some of the coefficients above assumed to be known are stochastic[183]. Current solution algorithms for MSPs are not capable of using continuous distributions of stochastic variables, therefore a proper discretization of the originally assumed or estimated distributions has to be performed[184]. Sub-chapter 4.2.3 deals with this issue.

Further deviations from the original formulation of a linear program might be an objective function that is nonlinear. This lies in the nature of the possible objective criteria[185]. Some solvers available are nevertheless capable of solving such programs with nonlinear objective function and linear constraints[186].

An important restriction that has to hold for the MSP is non-anticipativity, or in other words implementability[187]. This refers to the realistic assumption, that information about future developments is not known and therefore should not influence the decision of the present. For the optimization this means that two different scenarios that have a common history must have made the same decisions (portfolio reinvestments) up to the point in time when their paths diverged[188].

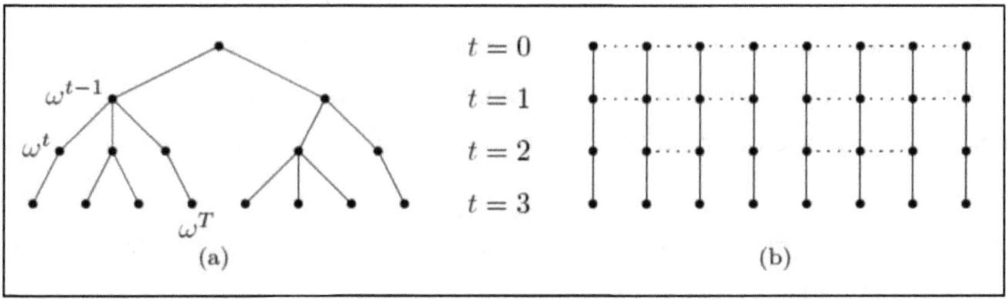

Figure 6: Scenario tree (a) and non-anticipativity constraints linking common history (b)[189]

[183] Kall/Mayer (2010), p. 2

[184] Cutaia (2007), p. 5

[185] Objective criteria mentioned in sub-chapter 4.1.1, like the Sharpe ratio or the standard deviation, are nonlinear functions.

[186] Dupačová et al. (2000), p. 28

[187] Zanjani et al. (2009), p. 6

[188] Frauendorfer/Schürle (2007), p. 13

[189] Cutaia (2007), p. 56

Figure 6 (b) illustrates that paths with a common history (as depicted in Figure 6 (a)) made the same decisions, which can be ensured by specified constraints in the optimization[190]. In the case study, however, non-anticipativity is implemented implicitly[191], by specifying only one variable for each decision (node). This reduces the size and complexity of the optimization problem.

4.2.1 Notation

In this sub-chapter the notations[192] for the necessary elements used in the following sub-chapters are shown.

$\mathcal{D}_t = \{1, \dots, \mathrm{D}\}$ represents all the maturities that exist in the replicating portfolio at time t, where D represents the maximum of the longest maturity in an initial portfolio and the currently maximum tradable maturity. Furthermore, $\mathcal{D}_t^S \subseteq \mathcal{D}_t$ defines the part of maturities that may be invested in, which refers to newly issued products. The elements of $\mathcal{D}_t$ are referred to as d in subscripts and superscripts.

For simplicity there are no bid-ask spreads considered, neither are restrictions on the market supply[193], assuming that the European wholesale funding market as well as the swap market has enough depth and liquidity to cover all necessary transaction of the replicating portfolio at the given market quotation[194].

The joint evolution of stochastic factors is represented by $\omega := (\omega_t; t = 1, \dots, T)$ in discrete time. ω contains the stochastic factor η_t for the Vasicek model as well as ξ_t for the volume evolution[195]. To comply with the above mentioned non-anticipativity, at each point in time t only the history and present $\omega^t := (\omega_1, \dots, \omega_t)$ is known.

The following coefficients depend at least indirectly on this stochastic process which is indicated in parentheses[196]:

---

[190] Frauendorfer/Schürle (2007), p. 13

[191] Zanjani et al. (2009), p. 7

[192] The notation is based on Frauendorfer/Schürle (2007), pp. 336-337 with some deviations due to simplifications and different model specifications.

[193] A horizontal supply curve for all financial products used in the model is assumed.

[194] The model could be extended for bid-ask spreads and artificial tranches that can be sold or borrowed each at the current rate plus a specific spread. For a practical application see Frauendorfer/Schürle (2007), pp. 336-339.

[195] For a more detailed description of the stochastic processes see Frauendorfer/Schürle (2007), p. 336.

[196] For simplicity the dependency notation with parentheses is skipped in the following use.

$r_t^d(\eta^t)$ rate at time t for investing or borrowing with time to maturity $d \in \mathcal{D}_t^S$

$c_t(\eta^t)$ client rate at time t paid for the non-maturing liability

$v_t(\omega^t)$ volume of the NMA

for time $t = 1, \dots, T$.

The values of the above depicted stochastic variables can be observed for time $t = 0$.

Decisions have to be made at the present and each time $t = 0, \dots, T$ until the end of the planning horizon T and have the following notation:

$x_t^{d,+}$ amount newly invested at time t with time to maturity $d \in \mathcal{D}_t^S$

$x_t^{d,-}$ amount newly borrowed[197] at time t with time to maturity $d \in \mathcal{D}_t^S$

x_t^S absolute surplus or margin (cash inflow of the replicating portfolio minus cash outflow of the NMA) at time t

The known variable x_{-1}^d[198] stands for the amounts invested with time to maturity $d \in \mathcal{D}_t$ one point in time before the decision for today is made (amounts of the initial portfolio). An interest cash flow cf_{-1}^d is received at maturity $d \in \mathcal{D}_t$ from each amount x_{-1}^d disregarding new investment or borrowings.

The nominal amounts x_{-1}^d of the initial portfolio are not calculated by the model and need to be derived by other means, e.g. a static model[199] or an expert opinion before the first application of the dynamic model.

4.2.2 Defining Constraints

The following constraints ensure compliance with the policies and specifications of the replicating portfolio mentioned in sub-chapter 4.1.

The constraints are formulated using the compact formulation suggested by Cutaia that requires less decision variables as well as fewer constraints and therefore reduces the complexity model[200].

[197] The restrictions defined in sub-chapter 4.2.3 do not allow for short positions, however to have a flexible model at hand, which could also deal with short position, this term will be included.

[198] The time index of -1 refers to an initial portfolio, from which the optimization starts.

[199] With the methodology for creating an initial portfolio as described in sub-chapter 4.1.1.

[200] Cutaia (2007), pp. 28-35

The first constraint makes sure that the total nominal amount invested in the replicating portfolio equals the volume of the NMA position at each time $t = 0, \dots, T$:

$$\sum_{\tau=0}^{t} \sum_{\substack{d \in \mathcal{D}_{t-\tau}^{S} \\ d>\tau}} x_{t-\tau}^{d,+} - \sum_{\tau=0}^{t} \sum_{\substack{d \in \mathcal{D}_{t-\tau}^{S} \\ d>\tau}} x_{t-\tau}^{d,-} = v_t - \sum_{d=t+2}^{D} x_{-1}^{d}$$

The first two terms represent sums of all newly invested or borrowed amounts up to time t that are not matured yet. The last term on the left side stands for all amounts of the initial portfolio that are still part of the portfolio at time t.

To comply with the investment policies of the above defined replicating portfolio, investment has to be restricted to amounts maturing in the current period at time $t = 0, \dots, T$:

$$\sum_{d \in \mathcal{D}_t^S} x_t^{d,+} - \sum_{\tau=1}^{t} \sum_{\substack{d \in \mathcal{D}_{t-\tau}^{S} \\ \tau \le d < m_t+\tau}} x_{t-\tau}^{d,+} + \sum_{\tau=1}^{t} \sum_{\substack{d \in \mathcal{D}_{t-\tau}^{S} \\ \tau \le d < m_t+\tau}} x_{t-\tau}^{d,-} \le \sum_{\substack{d=1 \\ t+d \le D}}^{m_t} x_{-1}^{t+d} + v_t - v_{t-1}$$

The left hand side consists of the newly invested amounts in the current stage minus amounts invested in previous periods that are not yet matured plus amounts borrowed in previous periods that are not yet matured. This should be smaller or equal[201] than the change in volume plus the amounts maturing in $d = 1, \dots, m_t$ from the initial portfolio (for the described investment policy $m_t = 1$ for $t = 0, \dots, T$ meaning that only amounts maturing in the current stage are reinvested).

The following constraints offer the opportunity to set absolute and relative bounds to maturity buckets by introducing $l_{j,t}^{l}$ and $l_{j,t}^{u}$ as lower and upper absolute amounts in the maturities $\mathcal{D}_{j,t}^{l}, j = 1, \dots, m_t^{l}$ and $\mathcal{D}_{j,t}^{u}, j = 1, \dots, m_t^{u}$. Moreover, $w_{j,t}^{l}$ and $w_{j,t}^{u}$ represent relative lower and upper limits (as share of the whole amount in the replicating portfolio) of the maturities $\mathcal{D}_{j,t}^{w,l}, j = 1, \dots, n_t^{l}$ and $\mathcal{D}_{j,t}^{w,u}, j = 1, \dots, n_t^{u}$ respectively. To keep the section short only the lower bound constraints are shown, as they might be considered more important from a liquidity point of view:

201 In the case study only maturing amounts are allowed to be reinvested. Under this policy the smaller and equal sign may be replaced by an equal sign, as we want to invest the whole amount at least for the minimum tenor of one month.

$$-\sum_{\tau=0}^{t} \sum_{\substack{d \in \mathcal{D}_{t-\tau}^{S} \\ d-\tau \in \mathcal{D}_{j,t}^{l}}} x_{t-\tau}^{d,+} + \sum_{\tau=0}^{t} \sum_{\substack{d \in \mathcal{D}_{t-\tau}^{S} \\ d-\tau \in \mathcal{D}_{j,t}^{l}}} x_{t-\tau}^{d,-} \leq \sum_{\substack{d=t+2 \\ d-t-1 \in \mathcal{D}_{j,t}^{l}}}^{D} x_{-1}^{d} - l_{j,t}^{l}$$

$$t = 0, \dots, T; j = 1, \dots, m_t^l$$

$$-\sum_{\tau=0}^{t} \sum_{\substack{d \in \mathcal{D}_{t-\tau}^{S} \\ d-\tau \in \mathcal{D}_{j,t}^{w,l}}} x_{t-\tau}^{d,+} + \sum_{\tau=0}^{t} \sum_{\substack{d \in \mathcal{D}_{t-\tau}^{S} \\ d-\tau \in \mathcal{D}_{j,t}^{w,l}}} x_{t-\tau}^{d,-} \leq \sum_{\substack{d=t+2 \\ d-t-1 \in \mathcal{D}_{j,t}^{w,l}}}^{D} x_{-1}^{d} - w_{j,t}^{l} * v_t$$

$$t = 0, \dots, T; j = 1, \dots, n_t^l$$

As mentioned before the model applied in this thesis does not allow for short positions. That can be easily incorporated by setting appropriate relative or absolute lower or upper bounds[202]. Moreover, all the above depicted amounts borrowed $x_t^{d,-}$ can be omitted.

To calculate the surplus of the NMA the products in the replicating portfolio are assumed to be interest bearing, paying coupons at each period even if the product might actually be a zero bond[203]. Moreover, the constant α_0 is introduced to represent relative non-interest costs plus a profit margin[204] of the NMA[205]. When the objective criterion is the minimization of the absolute deviation from the NMA costs plus a margin, it might make sense to calculate sensitivities of the final outcome with respect to different margin targets. However, such a margin target is a management decision and a higher target will most probably increase the duration of the replicating portfolio in a normal yield curve regime. The surplus x_t^S at time $t = 0, \dots, T$ is then defined by the interest payments in the next period from products newly invested or borrowed due to the decision up until time t plus the interest payments in the next period from products in the portfolio as a remainder of the initial portfolio cf_{-1}^{t+2}:

$$x_t^S - \sum_{\tau=0}^{\min\{t,D-1\}} \sum_{\substack{d \in \mathcal{D}_{t-\tau}^{S} \\ d>\tau}} (x_{t-\tau}^{d,+} * r_{t-\tau}^{d} - x_{t-\tau}^{d,-} * r_{t-\tau}^{d}) = -(c_t + \alpha_0) * v_t + cf_{-1}^{t+2}$$

[202] Frauendorfer/Schürle (2007), p. 337-338

[203] Frauendorfer/Schürle (2007), p. 338

[204] Administration, Marketing, etc.

[205] Frauendorfer/Schürle (2007), p. 338

4.2.3 Defining the Objective Criterion

Objective functions to be optimized might be specified in several ways with differing implicit strategic focus but they limited by the required linearity. One might aim to maximize the overall expected income by minimizing the negative (expected) surplus[206]:

$$\min\ E^P\left(\sum_{t=0}^{T} -x_t^S\right)$$

Especially in risk management applications the aim is rather to stabilize income and limit the risk of (downside) deviations. The minimization of the absolute deviations from the client rate plus non-interest costs can be achieved by first introducing the auxiliary variable x_t^Mdefined by[207]:

$$-x_t^M - c_t^D * x_t^S \leq 0 \qquad t = 0, \ldots, T$$

$$-x_t^M + c_t^U * x_t^S \leq 0 \qquad t = 0, \ldots, T$$

The constants c_t^D and c_t^U are both one for the case of minimizing all absolute deviations, but might be specified as one and zero, for minimizing only downside deviations[208]. The objective function in both cases is:

$$\min\ E^P\left(\sum_{t=0}^{T} x_t^M\right)$$

Other before mentioned objective criteria as the standard deviation or the Sharpe ratio are hard to implement as a linear objective and for the sake of not making the optimization overly complex they are not applied in this case study.

4.2.4 Scenario Generation

To make MSPs tractable it is crucial to reduce complexity by proper discretization procedures for the originally continuous distributions of the stochastic variables used in the model.

In scientific literature on multistage stochastic programming it is therefore one of the major issues to find algorithms for creating scenario trees that contain as much information as possible of the original distributions by using only a few (probability weighted) scenarios.

206 See Cutaia (2007), p. 26 for a similar formulation.

207 See Cutaia (2007), p. 26 for a similar formulation.

208 For the latter see Frauendorfer/Schürle (2007), p. 339.

For the case study a practically quite simple approximation of the original distributions is used, which is based on the binomial distribution. Siede[209] demonstrates a methodology for creating a multinomial distribution that approximates the originally assumed multivariate normal distribution. His methodology is the basis for the scenario generation in this thesis. The main theoretical assumption behind this approximation is the central limit theorem and its ("reverse") application to a binomially distributed random variable: Given a sufficiently high number of trials the outcomes converge to a normal distribution.

As this idea might also be applied to multivariate distributions, it provides a way for discretising multivariate normal distributions (including the bivariate distribution in this thesis).

The distributions of the stochastic factors η_t (Vasicek model) and ξ_t (volume evolution) are assumed to be non-correlated and following a multivariate normal distribution. Assuming non-correlation makes sense in this application, as the correlations between market rates and volumes are already taken into account by the regression parameters in the volume model. ξ_t then represents uncertainty that is not covered by the regression parameters. η_t and ξ_t have an expected value of zero represented by the mean vector $\mu' = (0{,}0)$. η_t has a standard deviation of one, whereas ξ_t has a standard deviation of 4,8 % of the total NMA volume (calculated from the residuals of the OLS estimation procedure in 3.3.3) represented by the covariance-variance matrix $\Sigma = \begin{pmatrix} 1 & 0 \\ 0 & 0{,}048 \end{pmatrix}$.

The methodology now is as follows:

- Some outcomes of a multinomial distribution are selected by a certain method, so that the expected values, variances, and covariances are known.
- Then these outcomes are multiplied with a certain transformation matrix, resulting in uncorrelated outcomes (variance – covariance has the form of a diagonal matrix) with means zero.
- Next the outcomes are divided by their standard deviation to generate a multinomially distributed random variable that represents an approximated multinomial standard normal distribution.

209 Siede (2000), pp. 145-149

- By multiplying the distributions with the assumed covariance matrix and adding the mean vector possible scenarios that have a known probability can be created.

Frauendorfer and Schürle have found this method of creating a scenario tree to be sufficiently accurate[210].

In the two-dimensional case, as it is applied in this thesis, the outcomes might be interpreted as coordinates in a three-dimensional room that lie on a plane[211]. By rotating the outcomes within this plane (via different transformation matrices), different sets of possible approximations might be generated. For the case study 12 different scenario sets of 2*3 (three for each stochastic factor) scenarios each are generated, and for each stage of the MSP one scenario set is randomly chosen (by a random draw from a uniform distribution).

The methodology is now depicted in further detail[212], using the notation of Cutaia[213].

Define a probability space $(\Omega, \mathcal{P}(\Omega), \mathrm{M})$, where $M = (B_0, \ldots, B_n)$ for n different stochastic factors, and a multinomial distribution with parameters $\left(m, \frac{1}{n+1}, \ldots, \frac{1}{n+1}\right)$. This will finally generate $\binom{m+n}{n}$ [214] scenarios. Deciding for a parameter m and with it the number of scenarios, one has to bear in mind that the number of scenarios rises up to the power of the total number of stages[215].

The possible outcomes of the distributions are defined by $n + 1$ integer values in the range of 0 to $n + 1$, where the sum of them must equal the parameter m:

$$\Omega = \left\{ (\omega_0, \ldots, \omega_n) \in \mathbb{N}_0^{n+1} | \sum_{i=0}^{n} \omega_i = m \right\}$$

The probability of these outcomes is then defined by:

$$P(\omega_0, \ldots, \omega_n) := \frac{m!}{\prod_{i=0}^{n} \omega_i!} * \left(\frac{1}{n+1}\right)^m$$

---

210 Frauendorfer/Schürle (2007), p. 351

211 As depicted in Siede (2000), p. 146, and Cutaia (2007), p. 63.

212 For background information on multinomial distributions that is omitted here it is referred to Cutaia (2007), pp. 59-66, and Balakrishnan/Nevzorov (2003), pp. 49-62.

213 Cutaia (2007), pp. 61-62

214 This is to be interpreted as $m + n$ choose n, the binomial coefficient.

215 E.g. an m parameter of one combined with two stochastic factors results in three scenarios per stage. An MSP with six stages leads to a total amount of $3^6 = 729$ scenarios.

From the properties of multinomial distributions we can say that these $n+1$ binomial distributions $B_0, \dots, B_n$ all have the expected value of $E(B_i) = \frac{m}{n+1}$, a variance of $\sigma^2 = \frac{m*n}{(n+1)^2}$ and a covariance between each of them of $cov(B_i, B_j) = \frac{-m}{(n+1)^2}$. As the outcomes Ω might be interpreted as coordinates in an n+1 dimensional space, one can obtain n uncorrelated outcomes by multiplying the outcomes with a matrix that performs an orthogonal transformation. This matrix $T \in \mathbb{R}^{(n+1)\times((n+1)}$ with the elements $T_{i,j}; i,j = 0, \dots, n$ has the following entries:

$$T_{i,j} = \begin{cases} \sqrt{\frac{1}{n+1}} & i = 0; j = 0, \dots, n \\ \sqrt{\frac{n-i+1}{n-i+2}} & i > 0; j = i-1 \\ \sqrt{\frac{1}{(n-i+1)*(n-i+2)}} & i > 0; j \geq i \\ 0 & i > 0; j < i-1 \end{cases}$$

The orthogonalized distributions $\tau = T * B_i; i = 0, \dots, n$ then have the following properties:

- $P\left(\tau_0 = \frac{m}{\sqrt{n+1}}\right) = 1$, meaning that the distribution $T * B_0$ is only one point with mean of $\frac{m}{\sqrt{n+1}}$ and variance of 0.
- The means for all other distributions $i = 1, \dots, n$ are equal to 0, so the first moment already matches the standard normal distribution.
- The variances of these distributions are $\sigma^2 = \frac{m*n}{(n+1)^2}$, so we need to divide these distributions $\tau_i; i = 1, \dots, n$ by σ to get a variance of 1.
- The covariance $cov(\tau_i, \tau_j) = 0 \; \forall i,j = 1, \dots, n; i \neq j$, meaning the distributions are already uncorrelated.

So as mentioned we get a discrete distribution $x_i; i = 1, \dots, n$ that approximates the multivariate standard normal distribution by:

$$x_i = \sqrt{\frac{n+1}{m}} * \tau_i \, ,$$

which can now be scaled to the assumed distributions in the thesis:

$$X' := \sqrt{\Sigma} * X + \mu$$

X' now represents one possible scenario set that might be used for the simulation of the risk factor models in the MSP framework.

The output has (for two stochastic factors) to form of coordinates in a three dimensional room, were one axis value is constant, another axis represents the first and the remaining axis the second stochastic factor.

Furthermore, to add more variability and uncertainty to this approximation, different scenario sets might be generated by the above mentioned rotation of the outcomes in the plane. For the bivariate distribution in the case study, this can be done by multiplying the transformation matrix T from the left side with a matrix

$$D = \begin{pmatrix} \cos(\alpha) & \sin(\alpha) \\ -\sin(\alpha) & \cos(\alpha) \end{pmatrix},$$

where α is an arbitrary angle[216]. For the case study 12 scenario sets are created, one for each 10 degree rotation.

Figure 7 illustrates the structure of the generated scenario tree (for an MSP with six scenarios per stage), which is used in the case study. It is observable that there are more scenarios simulating rising rates (higher density of scenarios in the upper part as compared to the lower part of the scenario tree at stage three). This is due to the models mean reversion to the above calculated long term mean of 2,01%.

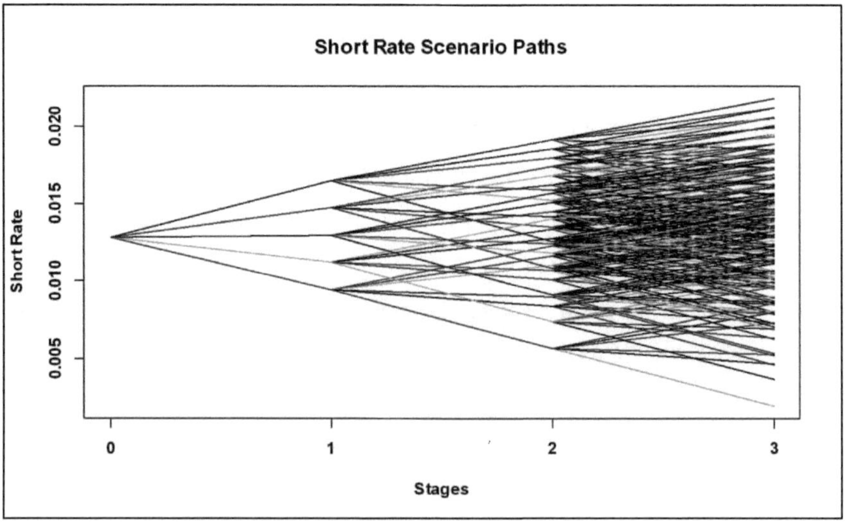

Figure 7: Market rate scenario tree

216 Considering the structure of this multivariate distribution in the plane (equilateral and equiangular triangle) it becomes obvious that exactly the same scenario set occurs after each 120 degree rotation. Thus, it only makes sense to rotate in the range from 0 to 120 degrees.

4.3 Implementation of the Program

Given that a suitable initial portfolio already exists the following steps need to be implemented to develop software that is capable of producing the desired output[217]:

- Firstly, all risk factor models are calibrated with the procedures introduced in chapter three.
- Secondly, stochastic factor scenarios are generated by the above mentioned scenario generation procedure (Appendix I).
- Then risk factor scenarios are simulated by applying the stochastic factor scenarios to the calibrated risk factor models.
- Thereafter, the scenario probabilities of each scenario in each stage are calculated (Appendix J).
- For the construction of the linear program, in particular the constraints; cash flows from the initial portfolio in the following periods need to be calculated[218] (Appendix K). However, this procedure needs initial weights as an external input, and is only necessary at its first use. For the continuous usage of the model the currently fixed nominal and interest cash flow schedules over the future periods only need to be updated with the new investment, which is extracted from the model output.
- To be able to solve the optimization problem a freely available external solver is used. However, this program requires data input in a specific form. Therefore, procedures need to be developed to generate this data. Preferably, the objective function is generated first (Appendix L). Here the solver requires a vector of coefficients. For the simplified model applied for the thesis, it consists of zeros for all decision variables that stand for investments in eligible products. Depending on the objective criterion the auxiliary variables that stand for the surplus x_t^S or the absolute deviations from the NMA costs plus margin x_t^M have entries equal to their corresponding scenario's (unconditional) probability.

217 In parentheses it is referred to the location (in the appendix) of R-procedures, which perform the required task.

218 See sub-chapters 4.2.1. and 4.2.1.

- Next, a right hand side vector of constants is calculated using the right hand sides of the above described constraints (Appendix M). In this thesis, first the constraints one to three are alternately implemented, followed by blocks of the fourth constraint and the auxiliary constraints (for x_t^M).
- The largest single procedure is the calculation of the left hand side matrix (Appendix N). This matrix has one or minus one as value for each element included in a constraint (as depicted above by the sums) and zeros everywhere else. Only some coefficients of the fourth constraint have different entries, representing the yields for the available products.
- In addition, a vector of operators is created, which consist of the elements "<=" and "=" (included in the left hand side matrix procedure in Appendix N).
- Finally, the solver applies a solving algorithm to the provided problem, resulting in optimal values for the decision variables with respect to the objective criterion (Appendix O). The most interesting outputs are the values for the optimal reinvestment at time $t = 0$ and the objective function value.

5 Model Output and Performance Analysis

The output of the model should be the optimal amounts (theoretically) invested today, to achieve the objective criterion in the future. The dynamically modelled replicating portfolio can then be included in risk management systems of the bank, especially in interest rate risk and liquidity risk management of NMAs. Furthermore, the yield of this portfolio can serve as the internal FTP for funds raised or products sold in the form of NMAs.

This chapter deals with analyses of the models performance and a comparison with the outcomes of a static approach. Additionally, outcomes of different parameter settings, especially different objective criteria, of the MSP are compared among each other to derive recommendations for superior settings.

5.1 Data Characteristics and Methodology

In this sub-chapter the main characteristics of the empirical environment as well the methodology of the performance analysis is pointed out to be able to interpret the outcomes properly.

Previous empirical analyses[219] cover time periods from 1989 to 2004, use yearly stages for a several years simulation period, and apply a constant target margin of 200 bp. As the global environment might have changed by now, this case study helps to answer the question if the model works as well in (after-)crisis times. However, the applied optimization is done over monthly stages and therefore distinguishes it from those previous implementations, which use yearly stages. Apparently, in between those yearly stages these models pursue a static reinvestment policy. Compared to them, a considerable disadvantage of the applied model is the fact that the simulation period is substantially shorter and at least one product is used, which lies outside the simulation period[220].

Another important difference is the strict abandonment of financing transactions, which has been allowed for in the above mentioned analyses. This policy is due to the negative connotation of short sales in general in European societies since the most recent financial crisis, which started in 2007. Short selling activities have even been subject to legal restrictions or even prohibition in many European

[219] See Cutaia (2007), pp. 112-134 and Frauendorfer/Schürle (2007), pp. 351-355.

[220] This issue is further addressed in sub-chapter 5.4.

countries since the crisis started. Pursuing this policy yet leads to situations in which the MSP has no feasible solution[221].

The (real) data sample in this case study has the following features over the testing period:

- The out-of-sample data stretches from June 2011 to May 2012 and therefore covers 12 investment decisions to be made. Due to the fairly short time for a testing period, generalizations of some of the outcomes have to be made with special care.
- The yield curves throughout this period are normal in shape. However, the level of the market rates falls continuously (basically shifting down in parallel). Short term rates even fall below client rates in the last three months of the testing period.
- Client rates remain at a similar low level at all points in time.
- The NMA volume shows a steady decrease for each month down to 75% of the starting value.
- The initial portfolio ranges back 60 months to periods of substantially higher interest rate levels.

The falling interest rate levels combined with maturing high yielding products and a stable client rate will inevitably cause a decline in the total margin of the portfolio.

The performance analysis methodology for the dynamic model irrespective of the particular model settings is as follows:

- Each (re-)investment decision fixes the return for the following period (one month).
- An initial portfolio is given as external input derived from the static model (with the same model settings as described below) for May 2011 and has the following composition: 29,06 % invested in the one month product, 19,68 % equally spread from one to three months maturity in the three month product, and 51,26 % equally spread from one to sixty months in the five year product.

[221] This issue is further addressed in sub-chapter 5.2.3.2.

- At each point in time a whole model run is performed, including calibration procedures with increased sample observations up to the current time and portfolio weights updated with maturing amounts and new investment.
- The return is calculated from the fixed portfolio return in the month minus the payments to clients and then divided by the current NMA Volume. The return is then shown in an annualized measure.
- Due to computational and memory restrictions[222] only six stages (six months) are implemented for a simulation period as the basic specification. Different numbers of stages are discussed in sub-chapter 5.4.

A very crucial conclusion from this introduction to the methodology and the data structure is that the initial investment of 50% in the five year product strongly limits the models range for action. This is due to the fact that the total NMA volumes decline at an even faster rate than the amounts in the five year product mature, causing a "natural" increase in the relative amount of these products. The dynamic model therefore suggests reinvestment primarily in short term products.

5.2 Comparing Static and Dynamic Model

To be able to benchmark the dynamically modelled replicating portfolio, a static model is applied as well. The outcome of this model is also used as the initial portfolio of the dynamic model. As both models will have the same initial weights, differences in their performance will become visible more and more with each period after the first calculation of the initial portfolio. This is caused by the forward looking dynamic model that will provide different portfolio weights for the reinvestment of maturing principal amounts.

After comparing the different outputs of the models, also the defects of both models are presented in further detail.

5.2.1 Static Model

The static model features the same investment policy described under point 4.1.1. The main differences to the dynamic model are:

- The objective criterion is the minimization of the standard deviation of the replicating portfolio margin throughout the sample period as compared to

[222] This issue is further discussed in sub-chapter 5.8.

the minimum weighted absolute deviation from a previously defined margin over simulated scenarios in the future.

- It takes only the historical scenario as input, whereas the dynamic model makes use of numerous future scenarios.
- The static model does not take the possibility of future changes in the reinvestment strategy into account.
- A static model in general needs liquidity restrictions in the form of lower limits for short time buckets, otherwise it tends to put too much weight on long term products. The dynamic model handles liquidity implicitly by incorporating scenarios of declining volumes, which are required to be feasible in the linear program. The minimum requirements are chosen to be approximately in line with the minimum simulated volumes in the dynamic model over six months in the future: The amounts maturing in one month have a minimum relative limit of 25 % of the total NMA volume and the ones maturing in three and six months of 15 % and 10% respectively. The cumulative percentages of all maturing amounts are used to ensure the fulfilment of these requirements[223].

If the new weights suggested by the static model cannot be achieved by reinvesting the maturing principals plus the volume change some positions need to be (fictively) unwound. This is discussed in sub-chapter 5.1.2.2.

5.2.2 Results

5.2.2.1 Evaluating Suitable Performance Figures

Firstly, the different meanings of the outputs of the models have to be highlighted. The output of the static model shows:

- An objective function value, which represents the minimized standard deviation of the portfolio margins over the calibration period (January 2009 until the current date).
- Decision variables, which stand for the weights for different products (maturities) in the portfolio. These optimal weights, when held static over the whole sample period, would have produced returns with the smallest standard deviation.

[223] E.g. more than 50 % of the whole portfolio invested in the one month product would already cover all minimum requirements for longer maturities.

The output of the dynamic model shows:

- An objective function value, which represents the minimized weighted absolute deviation from simulated NMA costs plus a predefined margin over the whole simulation period, taking into account the possibility of changes in weights after each stage. This value can be interpreted as the expected absolute deviation from the mentioned cost plus margin. However, there is no knowledge about the underlying distribution of this deviation from the predetermined value, which makes this objective function value statistically rather worthless other than for comparing it to the same model. Furthermore, the definition shows that this value is not a proper measurement for a comparison with the one from the static model.
- Decision variables, which mostly represent absolute amounts of reinvestments of free funds in different products (maturities) at each stage for each scenario. Furthermore, some of them stand for the actual or the absolute deviations from the simulated NMA costs plus the predefined margin.

To compare results from those conceptually different models, the outputs are brought in line by first representing both as the portfolio composition at each month. From that composition a margin (portfolio return minus interest payments to clients) of the portfolio is calculated for the specific month. The average margin over the testing period and its standard deviation is then compared to check for superior outcomes.

5.2.2.2 Comparing Performance Figures

Table 6 shows the performance figures for the static model and several dynamic model outputs with different settings[224]. The dynamic model apparently features substantially smaller standard deviations. In addition to this more stable margin, there is also one model setting that dominates the static model in both categories[225]. This is even more remarkable, when the model defects of the static model are considered, which basically overestimate the static models returns[226].

---

[224] The setting "UpDown" refers to an objective criterion that minimizes up- and downside deviations, whereas "Down" minimizes only the latter. See sub-chapter 5.3 for an explanation.

[225] More details to superior model settings are shown in the later sub-chapters.

[226] Next sub-chapter will elaborate on that notion.

Performance Figures (Static Model Benchmark)			
	Av. Margin	Stand. Dev.	Defects*
Dyn. Model 3scen/6stages/UpDown/160bp/4prod	1,769%	0,119%	0
Dyn. Model 3scen/6stages/UpDown/170bp/4prod	1,821%	0,064%	2
Dyn. Model 3scen/6stages/Down/160bp/4prod	1,883%	0,125%	0
Dyn. Model 3scen/6stages/Down/170bp/4prod	1,875%	0,128%	0
Static Model	1,848%	0,178%	6

* Dyn.: No Feasible Solution/Stat.: Investment Rule Violation

Table 6: Static vs. Dynamic model: Performance figures

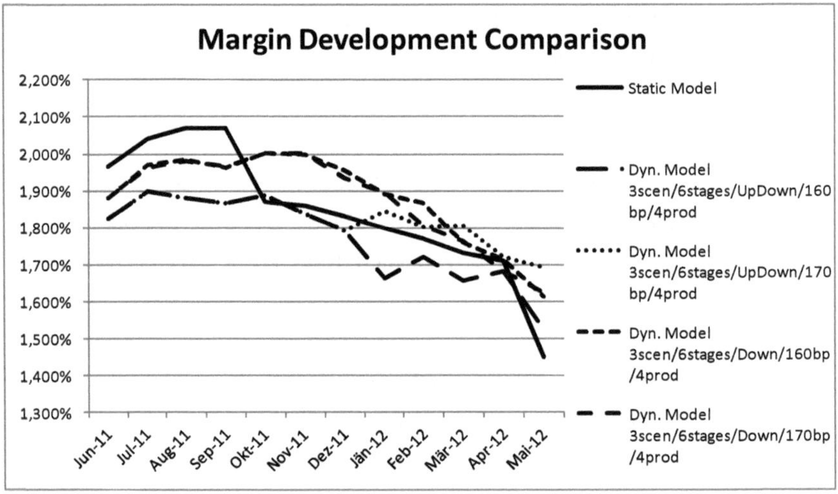

Figure 8: Static vs. Dynamic model margin development

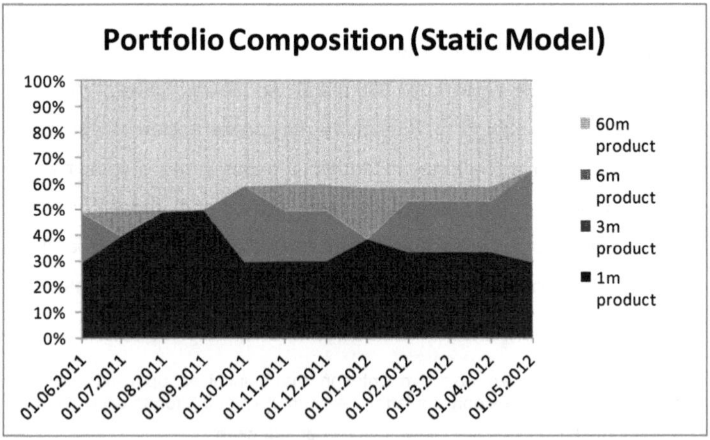

Figure 9: Static model portfolio composition

The margin evolution graph (Figure 8) shows the dynamic models' superior stability at the end of the testing period.

A graphical representation of the static model's weights (Figure 9) throughout the testing period shows that it puts much less weight on the five year product, therefore yielding lower margins. However, the dynamic models growing share of the five year product (Figure 10) is due to the decrease in volume, which is higher than the amounts maturing in this category. The model itself, does not suggest any further investment in the long term product in these settings.

Furthermore, it has to be emphasized that the dynamic models' output is at all times practically realizable without short sales.

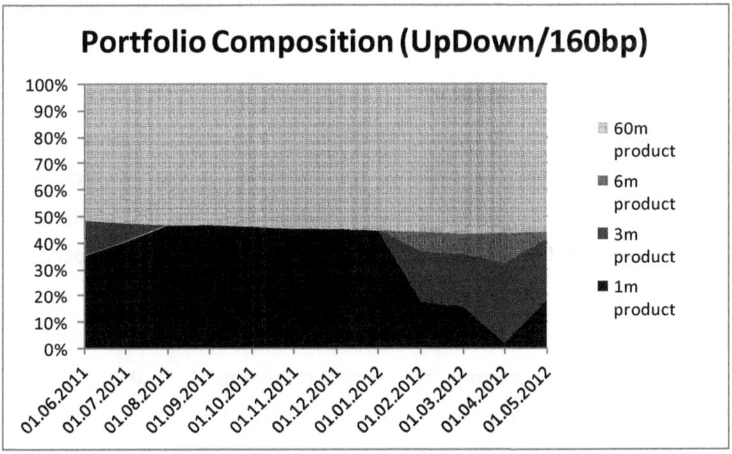

Figure 10: Dynamic model base settings & UpDown/160bp portfolio composition

5.2.3 Model Defects

Both models are subject to defects in some settings, which are further discussed in this sub-chapter.

5.2.3.1 Investment Rule Violations

The static model optimizes for each period a new composition of the whole replicating portfolio independent from the previous periods' weights or the currently maturing amounts. Thus, it might be the case that the current optimal portfolio composition cannot be achieved by (theoretically) reinvesting solely maturing amounts. This might happen even if only one more observation is added to the data sample on which the model is calibrated, as it frequently is the case in this performance analysis: The weights calculated at the end of July 2011, August 2011, October 2011, January 2012, February 2012, as well as May 2012 cannot be achieved by reinvesting only maturing amounts. This shows that the static model produced an investment rule violation in every second point in time in the testing period. For a real investment this would mean that some products need to be sold prematurely, which adds a considerable amount of (primarily) interest rate risk to the return of this portfolio. Moreover, it clearly contradicts the consensus in scientific literature of keeping (theoretical) transaction cost of the replicating portfolio as low as possible. Even though those costs are fictive, the margin of the static portfolio is definitely overstated, and so would be derived FTP prices. For real hedging decisions based on the outcome of the static model, this issue might as well return real losses.

5.2.3.2 Missing Feasible Solution

The MSP, when set up correctly, does not produce such an outcome at all, meaning that any output from the MSP is per definition investable from the currently maturing amounts. However, it might happen that the linear program might not be solvable in the first place. This happens when contradictions occur in the constraints.

In the set up as it is presented in this thesis contradictions may occur with the minimum (or, when applied, maximum) weight requirement in the following situation: The maximum simulated volume decline (as absolute number) plus the minimum weight requirement at a future period of the simulation is higher than all maturing amounts up to the point in time when the minimum occurs. This means the model cannot possibly cover this volume decline, even when investing solely in the one month product.

This shows the major importance of the volume model in the MSP framework: If it is simulating extreme decline scenarios, even though they might be highly improbable, it causes the linear program to return an infeasible result[227]. This result might still look like a reasonable investment decision. However, it is just the last state of the iteration algorithm before the constraints first contradicted each other and it must not be used without careful consideration. If no different solution

[227] An attempt for remedy of this problem has been implemented in the volume scenario generation procedure (Appendix F) and is outlined in sub-chapter 3.3.1.

can be found, the best alternative is then always to invest the total maturing amount in the shortest time bucket, as this would come closest to the liquidity requirement[228].

What can be seen from this characteristic is the fact that the dynamic model first tries to cover all possible outflows and minimum weight requirements including the worst case. Only free funds are then allocated to optimally satisfy the objective criterion.

5.3 Comparing Different Objective Criteria

In this sub-chapter two main objective criteria[229] are compared:

- The minimization of the absolute deviation from predefined costs plus a margin.
- The maximization of the surplus over the predefined costs plus a margin throughout the simulation period.

Additionally, the minimization will be carried out with different treatment for upside deviations. Concretely, the weights 100 % and 0% are applied. A zero weight for upside deviations should cause more desired outcomes (less probability of not earning costs plus margin). However, it might increase the standard deviation of the outcomes. In addition, a zero weight for upside deviations will produce a meaningful objective value, as it subsequently can be interpreted as the expected downside deviation.

On the other hand, the maximization of the income should trigger more investment in higher rate products, as it is the primary goal to generate the highest interest cash flow right after fulfilling all constraints.

Performance Figures (Different Objective Functions)			
	Av. Margin	Stand. Dev.	Defects*
Dyn. Model 3scen/6stages/UpDown/160bp/4prod	1,769%	0,119%	0
Dyn. Model 3scen/6stages/UpDown/170bp/4prod	1,821%	0,064%	2
Dyn. Model 3scen/6stages/MaxIncome/160bp/4prod	1,995%	0,092%	11
Dyn. Model 3scen/6stages/MaxIncome/170bp/4prod	2,003%	0,099%	11
Dyn. Model 3scen/6stages/Down/160bp/4prod	1,883%	0,125%	0
Dyn. Model 3scen/6stages/Down/170bp/4prod	1,875%	0,128%	0
			* No Feasible Solution

Table 7: Objective functions comparison: Performance figures

[228] This policy is implemented in the case study.

[229] As depicted in sub-chapter 4.2.3. and Cutaia (2007), pp. 26-27.

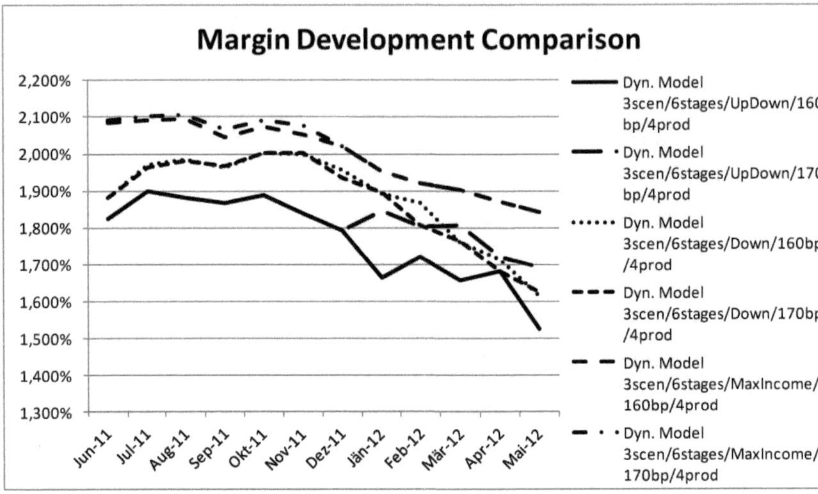

Figure 11: Objective function comparison: Margin development

At first sight, the income maximization seems to be the best objective function regarding both margin level and stability (Table 7 and Figure 11). However, the amount of infeasible solutions is very suspicious. Looking at the portfolio composition (Figure 12), the reason becomes obvious: A high investment in the five year product in period one causes liquidity problems for all subsequent stages. In this form, the portfolio composition is not acceptable from a liquidity point of view. As a remedy, maximum weight constraints for the long term products could be introduced.

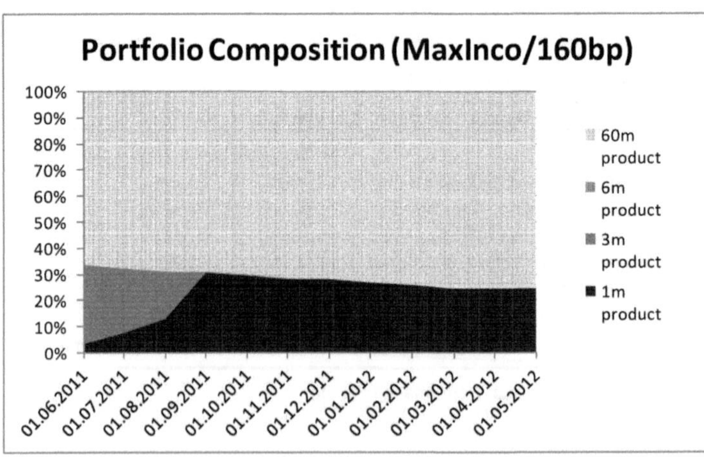

Figure 12: Dynamic model base settings & MaxIncome/160bp portfolio composition

Much more interesting for the purposes of this thesis is the difference between the two different minimization objective criteria. Here we see what was expected: Minimizing only downside deviations creates higher margins, however the standard deviation is slightly higher. The portfolio composition in Figure 13 shows a more sophisticated use of short term products as compared to the minimization in both directions (Figure10). Furthermore, the downside deviation objective criterion causes the least infeasible problems of all models.

These advantages together with the meaningful objective function value should make it the preferred model for practical applications.

A further counter-argument against the minimization of up- and downside deviations is that it might happen that e.g. 90 % of all deviations are upside deviations. In that case it is questionable if the model does any good by investing most of the free funds in the shortest maturity and therefore keeping the margin artificially low. The downside minimization is with this respect "closer to the market".

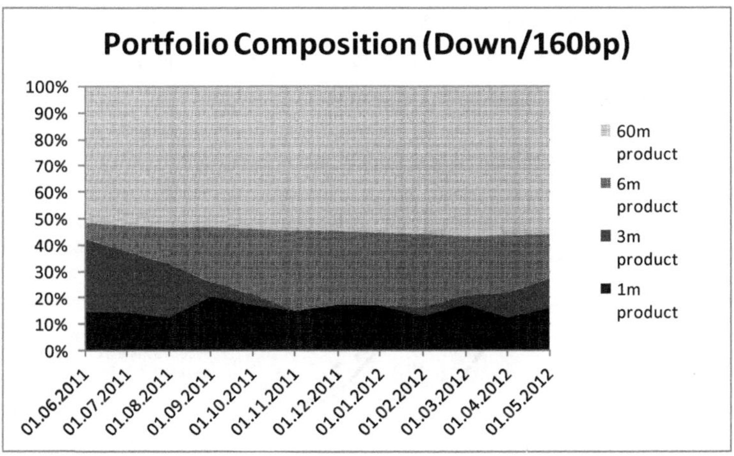

Figure 13: Dynamic model base settings & Down/160bp portfolio composition

5.4 Comparing Different Numbers of Stages

The number of stages is critical for the models capability of anticipating future changes in the main risk factors. More stages enable the model to meaningfully allocate money to products that mature before the maximum number of stages is reached. The model only allocates money to a product whose maturity exceeds the simulation period if there are free funds from a liquidity point of view and the objective criterion demands a higher rate (in the case of a normal yield curve, where rates of longer maturities have a higher level). However, the model does not "know" when these funds become available again, which is not a desired feature regarding liquidity risk in future periods. The latter might be the main reason, next to the actual volume decline, why the problem of no feasible solution when solving the linear program occurs in later periods of the performance analysis in many model settings.

Performance Figures (Different Number of Stages)			
	Av. Margin	Stand. Dev.	Defects*
Dyn. Model 3scen/6stages/UpDown/160bp/4prod	1,769%	0,119%	0
Dyn. Model 3scen/5stages/UpDown/160bp/4prod	1,763%	0,123%	1
Dyn. Model 3scen/6stages/Down/160bp/4prod	1,883%	0,125%	0
Dyn. Model 3scen/5stages/Down/160bp/4prod	1,853%	0,125%	0
			* No Feasible Solution

Table 8: Stage number comparison: Performance figures

Table 8 and Figure 14 show the superior performance when more stages are used. Figure 15 additionally depicts the fact, that the model allocates money only to products that either mature within the simulation horizon, or those which have the maximum (or theoretically also the minimum) yield.

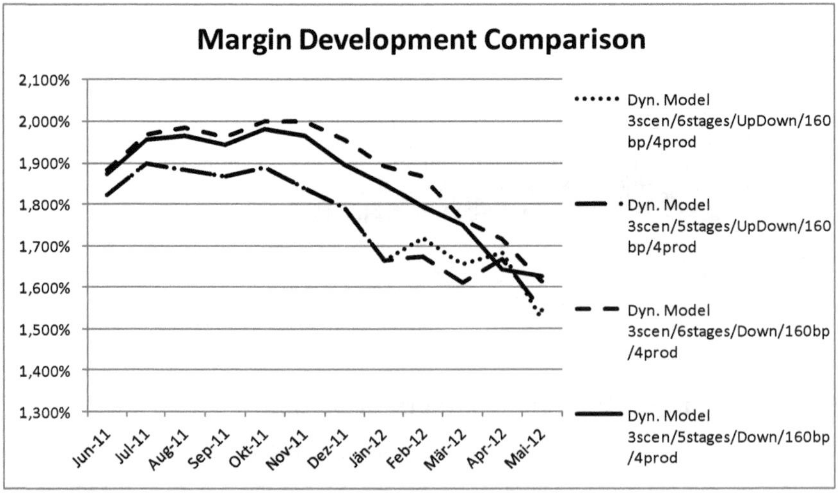

Figure 14: Stage number comparison: Margin development

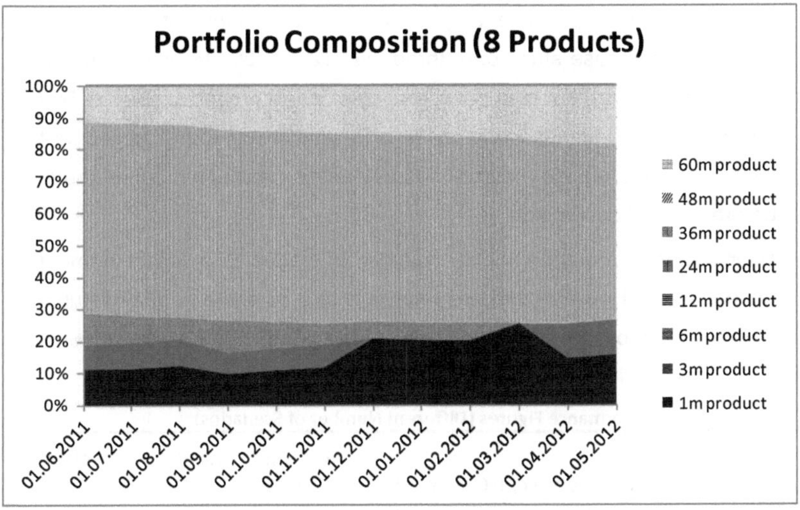

Figure 15: Dynamic model base settings & Down/160bp/8prod portfolio composition

The major block of the three years product in Figure 15 comes from a different initial portfolio calculated by the static model when eight products are available.

5.5 Comparing Different Numbers of Scenarios

In the scenario generation procedure an important (external) input is the factor m which basically defines the number of scenarios per stage. Fixing the number of required stochastic factors at two (as in the case study), an m of one, two, or three leads to three, six, or ten corresponding scenarios. Intuitively one would prefer a higher number of stages, as it should better fit the desired discretized normal distribution. However, as this is the basis which is taken to the power of the stage number to get to the amount of scenario nodes at the current stage, a lower scenario number is definitely preferred from a computational point of view. In other words, a higher number of scenarios per stage reduces the total number of stages, which is computationally possible. Since the number of stages should be as high as possible (as pointed out in chapter 5.3) and the number of scenarios is also preferred to be higher, the practitioner runs into some kind of dilemma. The principle that is applied in the case study is as follows:

- Firstly, attempt to implement as many stages as (computationally) possible by choosing the smallest m of one (three scenarios per stochastic factor).

- If the number of possible stages equals the maturity of an investable product (in the case study one, three, six, 12, 24, 36, 48, and 60 months), accept this setting. If it is in between two of those products, raise m by one and try if it is computationally possible to simulate as many stages so that all the products, whose maturity was below the maximum number of stages before, are still covered[230].

This principle clearly prefers a higher number of stages to a higher number of scenarios per stage. However, the assumption that a bivariate normal distribution is well approached by only three scenarios for each of the two distributions remains fairly optimistic[231].

Performance Figures (Different Number of Scenarios)			
	Av. Margin	Stand. Dev.	Defects*
Dyn. Model 3scen/6stages/UpDown/160bp/4prod	1,769%	0,119%	0
Dyn. Model 6scen/4stages/UpDown/160bp/4prod	1,785%	0,102%	3
Dyn. Model 3scen/6stages/Down/160bp/4prod	1,883%	0,125%	0
Dyn. Model 6scen/4stages/Down/160bp/4prod	1,935%	0,108%	10
			* No Feasible Solution

Table 9: Scenario number comparison: Performance figures

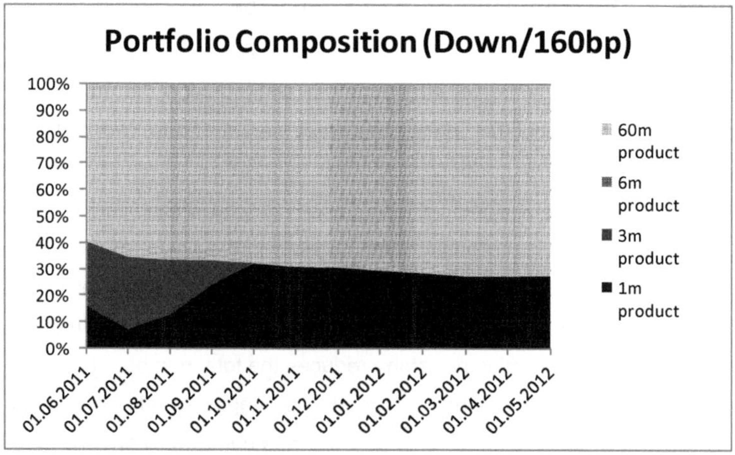

Figure 16: Dynamic model 6scen/4stages/Down/160bp/4prod portfolio composition

230 If the maximum possible number of stages is e.g. nine, the scenarios per stages should be raised. If the new maximum possible number of stages can cover a period of at least six months it should be preferred.

231 See Cutaia (2007), pp. 107-110, for a closer analysis of that issue.

Table 9 shows again that less stages cause problems with liquidity in later periods of the testing period. The superior performance figures come again from a too high investment in long term products and the subsequent liquidity shortages (no feasible solutions) as visible in Figure 16.

Additionally, the question if the outcome of a specific run is reliable or strongly dependent on the scenario generation procedures (stochastic factors) is answered by Figure 17: It shows that only minor deviations in the margins occur due to different random scenarios.

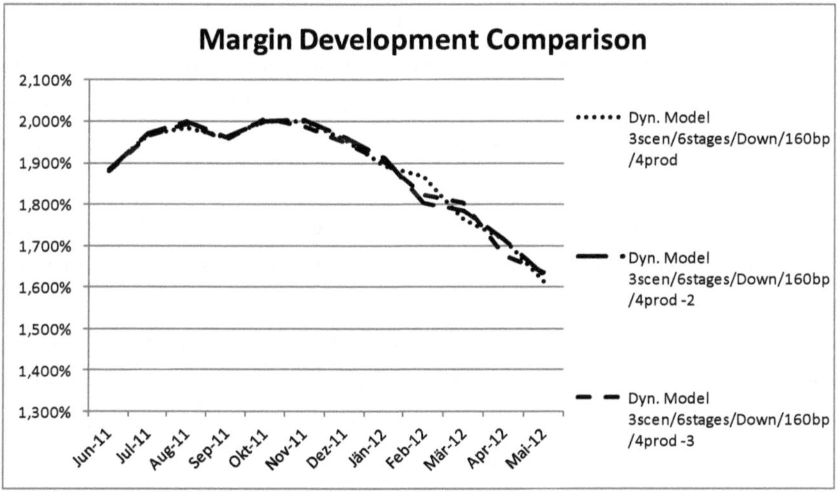

Figure 17: Margin development: Same settings, Different scenarios

5.6 Comparing Different Margin Levels

Another crucial model input is the value of non-interest costs plus a profit margin. On the one hand, the non-interest costs, which should basically cover all marketing and administration costs that can be allocated to the acquisition and continued servicing of the NMAs, should be calculated from bank internal data. For simplicity this value can be fixed for a period of time (e.g. a year).

On the other hand, a profit margin is to some extent an arbitrary value that could be fixed or variable. As mentioned above FTP prices can have a substantial influence on profit center results on both sides of the balance sheet, therefore special care has to be taken to find an objective and reasonable value.

The main drivers of the profit margin in times when client rates are on a constant low are past and current interest rate levels that together constitute the replicating portfolio return. The following notions might help to objectively narrow down the possible range of the total margin (including the non-interest costs):

- The currently maturing amount, which usually covers a substantial part of the total NMA volume has to be invested at current interest rate levels.
- The same can be said about amounts maturing in future stages of the simulation period, with the exception that the market rates exist only in the form of many different future scenarios.
- Past interest rates from products that have not yet matured contribute to the portfolio return. This part is fixed by investments in the past and has to be calculated for MSP constraints in the form of interest rate cash flows from the initial portfolio.

That means a considerable part[232] of the (simulated) return is already fixed from the beginning, whereas the other part is composed by current and future rates times the amounts of reinvestment in each period. The fixed part can be easily extracted from calculations that already exist for the MSP, in particular for the right hand side of the constraints. As the future scenarios of all risk factors as well as their probabilities (weights in the objective function) are known, an estimate for the current margin can be calculated by assuming reinvestment only in the one month product.

Yet, an economic rationale behind a target margin based solely on market data is hard to recognize.

Moreover, a variable margin that is based on the current expected yield in case of investing solely in the one month product turned out to be unsuitable, especially in times of falling interest rates:

- As the margin is bound to decline due to a general decline in interest rates, the current margin is a very ambitious target for the future stages. As a consequence, the model allocates money to longer maturities.

[232] Assuming a flat yield curve, an initial investment of 50 % in a five year product and a simulation period of six months, approximately 47 % of the interest cash flows throughout the simulation period are fixed only by the long term investment. Even more will be fixed if the other products are included in this calculation.

- This causes an increase in the margin today and as well for the (variable) margin for the next period, where it is even harder to achieve such a high return.

Under these circumstances the model runs almost immediately in liquidity problems. Therefore, a purely statistical choice of the variable margin is not recommended.

Performance Figures (Different Margin Levels)			
	Av. Margin	Stand. Dev.	Defects*
Dyn. Model 3scen/6stages/UpDown/150bp/4prod	1,737%	0,153%	0
Dyn. Model 3scen/6stages/UpDown/160bp/4prod	1,769%	0,119%	0
Dyn. Model 3scen/6stages/UpDown/170bp/4prod	1,821%	0,064%	2
Dyn. Model 3scen/6stages/UpDown/180bp/4prod	1,833%	0,065%	2

* No Feasible Solution

Table 10: Margin level comparison: Performance figures (UpDown)

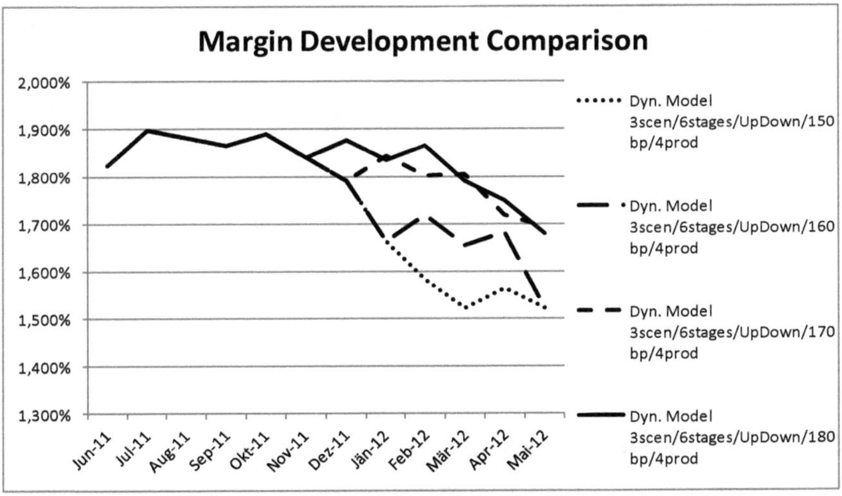

Figure 18: Margin level comparison: Margin development (UpDown)

Table 10 and 11 each compare the same model setting with different static margin levels. Here we can see another desired feature of the downside minimization objective criterion: It is stable over different margin levels (see also Figure 18 vs. Figure 19). Changing the target margin only causes a different number of downside deviations without virtually "forcing" it to push or pull the actual margin in one or the other direction.

On the other hand, the minimization of all deviations pulls the actual margin down at low target margin levels, whereas it produces liquidity problems, when a high target margin level has to be maintained.

Performance Figures (Different Margin Levels)			
	Av. Margin	Stand. Dev.	Defects*
Dyn. Model 3scen/6stages/Down/150bp/4prod	1,877%	0,121%	0
Dyn. Model 3scen/6stages/Down/160bp/4prod	1,883%	0,125%	0
Dyn. Model 3scen/6stages/Down/170bp/4prod	1,875%	0,128%	0
Dyn. Model 3scen/6stages/Down/180bp/4prod	1,873%	0,125%	0
			* No Feasible Solution

Table 11: Margin level comparison: Performance figures (Down)

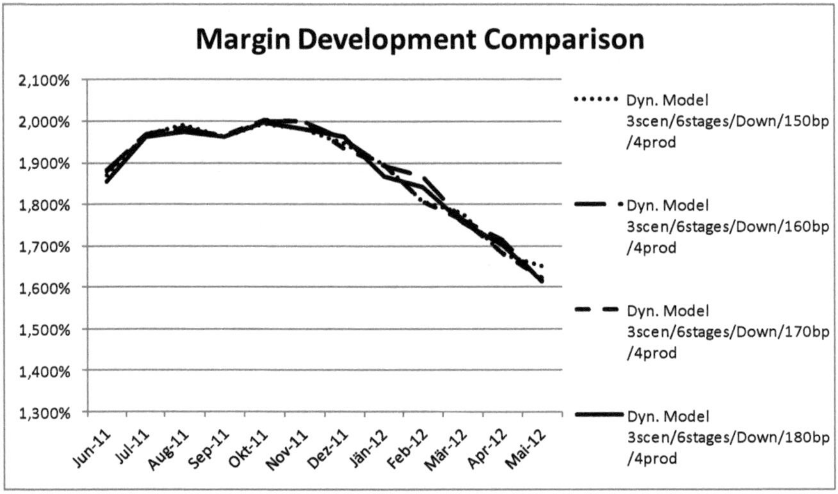

Figure 19: Margin level comparison: Margin development (Down)

5.7 Other Means of Validation

Bardenhewer outlines a basic back-testing procedure for a replicating portfolio from the field of interest rate risk management, which could be carried out to further test the quality of the model results[233]:

- Firstly, a present value of the replicating portfolio's cash flows is calculated for some point in time in the past.
- Secondly, key rates are shocked by small amounts and a key rate delta profile is derived.

[233] Bardenhewer (2007), pp. 247-248

- Thirdly, the key rate positions in the portfolio are hedged via forward rate agreements and interest rate swaps.
- In a near future point in time the present value of the portfolio plus the profit or loss on the hedge products is calculated and the deviation from the original present value plus the riskless interest rate is calculated.
- This procedure is applied for multiple time steps in a rolling window and should point out the models actual hedge effectiveness.

From a liquidity risk perspective it is interesting to know how the volume model performs out of sample. Here the expected and the minimum volume scenario might be of special interest in comparison with the actual development.

Furthermore, each of the risk factor models should undergo extensive validation procedures. This has been done only to a limited extent in this case study.

5.8 Computational Performance

The computational difficulty of the program in the form as it is depicted here lies solely with the generation and solution of the linear program. On the one hand, the solution of the linear program is the main driving factor of the computational time. On the other hand the matrix of coefficients on the left hand side of the linear program is the main restricting factor from a memory point of view. The latter is due to its exponentially increasing dimensions with each stage:

- The number of rows is calculated by the number of scenarios times the number of investable products plus two times the number of scenarios (for variables holding absolute deviations).
- The number of rows is calculated by multiplying the number of scenarios with the number of constraints plus two times the scenario number for the auxiliary constraints.
- The number of scenarios is calculated by adding up all stages, where each stage holds the basic number of scenarios to the power of the stage number.

In the base setting of the linear program with four investable products, three scenarios per stage, and six stages, this grows to a matrix with the dimensions of 6558x6558 holding 43 million entries. In R this matrix takes 328 megabytes of the computer's memory. One stage more, lets this value explode to six gigabytes.

Only with this huge problem sizes the computational time gets a problem. However, in the above mentioned base setting the entire model run (including calibration and scenario generation) lasts mere 75 seconds, which is a very practical length of time.

6 Conclusion and Outlook

The thesis gives a functioning example of how to structure an implementation of a dynamic model for the risk management and pricing of NMAs via the means of an MSP in the statistical programming language R. The latter is fully capable of carrying out all the necessary procedures from a statistical point of view.

The one factor Vasicek model is a practically manageable way the implement a TSM. However, as it is an integrated part in the scenario generation procedure as well as in the MSP, its limited capability of simulating all different kinds of empirically observable yield curve shapes gives room for improvement. On the other hand, the entire dynamic model has in any case a considerable amount of inherent uncertainty (or model risk) and therefore a parsimonious TSM is to prefer for practical purposes. If a more realistic TSM is demanded, it should be attempted to develop a model that simulates interest rates under the physical probability measure P[234] as opposed to ones in the risk-neutral measure.

The applied client rate model shows plausible outcomes, but runs into problems when it has to deal with small sample sizes and therefore low observation frequencies for different change categories. Alternatives are numerous and exhibit a similar degree of sophistication from both a theoretical and an application-oriented point of view[235].

The volume model turned out to be a crucial model element from a liquidity risk management point of view: By simulating severe decline scenarios the dynamic model might be even more restrictive than a static model with explicit liquidity restrictions. This is due to the characteristic of the linear program that even the most severe decline scenario must be feasible with the final output (current investment decision). Therefore the model invests considerable amounts in short maturities to be able to cover possible future declines in total volume. Considering its important role in the dynamic model framework a simple regression might be simplistic and future research on behavioural factors should help to develop more realistic NMA volume models[236].

234 E.g. extensions of the above mentioned Diebold-Li model.

235 For an overview on alternative models see Paraschiv/Frauendorfer (2011), pp. 5-7.

236 For the first application of a theory on client behavior in modeling NMA volumes see Nyström (2008), pp. 709-756.

The out-of-sample performance analysis leads to the following conclusions on the model parameters of the linear program:

- The higher the number of stages, the better the models foresight and the smaller the probability of infeasible solutions.
- Due to the same reason, a smaller amount of scenarios per stage is preferable, as it allows for a higher number of stages.
- In the ideal case the stages should at least equal the maturity of the longest investable product, so that the model "is aware" of the future liquidity implications of all of its investment decisions.
- To use products whose maturity is longer than the simulation horizon is not useful. One long term product can be added to incorporate a rate from the long end of the yield curve.
- The chosen non-interest service cost plus a margin become a less critical input, when only downside deviations are minimized.
- The margin can be adjusted regularly but not frequently to reflect current market interest rate levels.
- The initial portfolio can have a substantial influence on the results in the first year of usage. This is especially the case, when the initial portfolio has a large share of long term products.
- Minimizing only downside deviations is the most practical objective criterion.

As opposed to a static model, the dynamic model does not produce an output that violates the investment rules, but might return no solution. Although this defect is hard to avoid for any kind of situation, it does not mean that some of the investment rules are violated. In the general case, it rather indicates possible current or future liquidity problems of the replicating portfolio. Previous analyses avoided this problem by allowing for short sales.

A performance comparison with a static model over the out-of-sample data confirms previous findings of the superiority of the dynamic model even in the aftermath of the financial crisis and its persisting low interest rate regime: The returns over the sample period are basically identical on average in both models, whereas the standard deviation is significantly lower for the returns of the dynamic model. However, the returns of the static model are for all practical purposes substantially lower and more widely scattered considering the need to prematurely unwind open investment positions.

The data used in the case study covers only a quite limited time period and only savings accounts. Further empirical analyses with different kind of products and larger data samples are still needed to be able to generalize the outcomes of this case study.

To make the dynamic model more reliable the simulation period has to be extended as far as possible. This can be achieved by changing the scenario generation procedure, extending the period between investment decisions[237], or to a small extent by using very powerful hardware.

The thesis shows that dynamic modelling of NMAs via an MSP approach is a manageable alternative to a static approach, but takes qualified personnel for its development and operation. Especially the numerous, partly unintuitive, external inputs, model parameters, and outputs can cause errors or leave room for manipulation (in its worst connotation).

Finally, explaining the model to a possibly non-expert management remains a highly non-trivial task, particularly when even more sophisticated risk factor models are introduced.

[237] As applied by Cutaia (2007), pp. 112-134 and Frauendorfer/Schürle (2007), pp. 351-355.

7 Bibliography

Akaike, H. (1974): A new look at the statistical model identification, IEEE Trans. Automatic Control, Vol. 19, No. 6, pp. 716-23

Balakrishnan, N., and Nevzorov, V.B. (2003): A Primer on Statistical Distributions, Hoboken, New Jersey: Wiley

Bardenhewer, M.M. (2007): Modeling Non-maturing Products, In Matz, L., and Neu, P. (eds.), Liquidity Risk Measurement and Management: A Practitioner's Guide to Global Best Practices (pp. 220-256), Singapore: Wiley

Basel Committee on Banking Supervision (2010): Basel III: International framework for liquidity risk measurement, standards and monitoring, Bank for International Settlements, Basel

Basel Committee on Banking Supervision (2004): Principles for the management and supervision of interest rate risk, Bank for International Settlements, Basel

Basel Committee on Banking Supervision (2009): Range of practices and issues in economic capital frameworks, Bank for International Settlements, Basel

Bessis, J. (2010): Risk Management in Banking, 3rd ed., Chichester: Wiley

Björk, T. (2009): Arbitrage Theory in Continuous Time, 3rd ed., Oxford: Oxford University Press

Black, F., and Scholes M. (1973): The Pricing of Options and Corporate Liabilities, Journal of Political Economy, Vol. 81, No. 3, pp. 637-654

Blöchlinger, A. (2011): Management Framework for Non-Maturity Accounts: From the Marketing to the Hedging Strategy, Zürcher Kantonalbank

Bolder, D.J. (2006): Modelling Term-Structure Dynamics for Risk Management: A Practitioner's Perspective, Working Paper 2006-48, Bank of Canada

Chiburis, R., Lokshin, M. (2007): Maximum Likelihood and Two-Step Estimation of an Ordered-Probit Selection Model, The Stata Journal, Vol. 7, No.2, pp. 167-182

Cipu, E.C., Udriste, S. (2009): Estimating Non-Maturity Deposits, In Rudas, I., Demiralp, M., Mastorakis, N. (eds.), Proceedings of the 9th WSEAS International Conference on Simulation, modeling and optimization (pp. 369-374), Stevens Point: World Scientific and Engineering Academy and Society

Cochrane, D., Orcutt, G.H. (1949): Application of Least Squares Regression to Relationships Containing Auto-Correlated Error Terms, Journal of the American Statistical Association, Vol. 44, No. 245, pp. 32-61

Cox, J.C., Ingersoll, J.E., Jr., Ross, S.A. (1985): A theory of the Term Structure of Interest Rates, Econometrica, Vol. 53, No. 2, pp. 385-408

Cutaia, M. (2007): Szenariogenerierung in der mehrstufigen stochastischen Optimierung, Ph.D. Dissertation, University of St. Gallen

Dai, Q. and Singleton, K.J. (2000): Specification Analysis of Affine Term Structure Models, The Journal of Finance, Vol. 55, No. 5, pp. 1943-1978

Dantzig, G.B. (1963): Linear Programming and Extensions, Princeton: Princeton University Press

de Jong, F., Wielhouwer, J. (2003): The valuation and hedging of variable rate savings accounts, Astin Bulletin, Vol. 33 (2), 383-397

Dewachter, H., Lyrio, M., Maes, K. (2006): A multi-factor model for the valuation and risk management of demand deposits, Working paper – Research Series No 83, National Bank of Belgium

Diebold, F.X., Li, C. (2006): Forecasting the Term Structure of Government Bond Yields, Journal of Econometrics, Vol. 130, pp. 337-364

Duarte, J. (2004): Evaluating an Alternative Risk Preference in Affine Term Structure Models, The Review of Financial Studies, Vol. 17, No. 2, pp. 379-404

Duffee, G.D. (2002): Term Premia and Interest Rate Forecasts in Affine Models, Journal of Finance, Vol. 57, pp. 405-443

Duffie, D. (2001): Dynamic Asset Pricing Theory, Princeton: Princeton University Press

Dupačová, J., Consigli, G., Wallace, S. (2000): Scenarios for Multistage Stochastic Programs, Annals of Operations Research, Vol. 100, pp. 25-53

Dybvig, P.H., and Ross, S.A. (1987): Arbitrage, In Eatwell, J., Milgate, M., and Newman, P. (eds.), The New Palgrave Dictionary of Economics, (pp. 100-106), London: The MacMillan Press Ltd

Elliot, R.J., and Kopp, P.E. (1999): Mathematics of Financial Markets, New York: NY Springer-Verlag New York Inc

Ellis, D. M. and Jordan, J. V. (2001): The Evaluation of Credit Union Non-Maturity Deposits, National Economic Research Associates, prepared for National Credit Union Administration, Working Paper

Engle, R.F., Granger, C.W.J. (1987): Co-Integration and Error Correction: Representation, Estimation, and Testing, Econometrica, Vol. 55, No. 2, pp. 251-276

Entrop, O., Krombach, A., Memmel, C., Wilkens, M. (2009): Non-maturing Assets and Liabilities of Banks: Valuation and Risk Measurement, Working Paper

Fleten, S.E., Høyland, K., Wallace, S.W. (2001): The performance of stochastic dynamic and fixed mix portfolio models, European Journal of Operational Research, Vol. 140, pp. 37-49

Flood, M.D. (1991): An Introduction to Complete Markets, The Federal Reserve Bank of St. Louis Review, Vol. 73, No. 3, pp. 32-57

Forrest, B., Frauendorfer, K., Schürle, M. (1997). A Stochastic Optimization Model for the Investement of Savings Account Deposits, In Kischka et.al. (eds.), Operations Research Proceedings 1997 (382-387), Heidelberg: Springer-Verlag

Frauendorfer, K., Schürle, M. (2007): Dynamic modelling and optimization of non-maturing accounts, In Matz, L., and Neu, P. (eds.), Liquidity Risk Measurement and Management: A Practitioner's Guide to Global Best Practices (pp. 327-359), Singapore: Wiley

Frauendorfer, K., Schürle, M. (2000): Stochastic optimization in asset and liability management: A model for non-maturing accounts, In Uryasev, S.P. (ed.), Probabilitstic Constrained Optimization: Methodology and Applications (pp. 67-101), Norwell: Kluwer

Frauendorfer, K., Schürle, M. (2000): Term Structure models in multistage stochastic programming: estimation and approximation, Annals of Operations Research, Vol. 100, pp. 189-209

Hannan, T., Berger, A. (1991): The Rigidity of Prices: Evidence from the Banking Industry, American Economic Review, Vol. 81, pp. 938-945

Heath, D., Jarrow, R., Morton, A. (1992): Bond Pricing and the Term Structure of Interest Rates: A New Methodology, Econometrica, Vol. 60, No.1, pp. 77-108

Heidorn, T., Schmaltz, C. (2008): Neue Entwicklungen im Liquiditätsmanagement, In Bartetzky, P., Gruber, W., Wehn, C. (eds.), Handbuch Liquiditätsrisiko: Identifikation, Messung und Steuerung (pp. 193-229), Stuttgart: Schäffer-Poeschl Verlag

Huarong, T., Yihong, X. (2005): An International Examination of Affine Term Structure Models and the Expectations Hypothesis, Working Paper, University of Pennsylvania, Wharton School, The Rodney L. White Center for Financial Research

Hutchison, D. and Pennacchi, G. (1996): Measuring Rents and Interest Rate Risk in Imperfect Financial Markets: The Case of Retail Deposits, Journal of Financial and Quantitative Analysis, Vol. 31, pp. 399-417

James, J., Webber, N. (2000): Interest Rate Modelling, Chichester: Wiley

Janosi, T., Jarrow, R. and Zullo, F. (1999): An Empirical Analysis of the Jarrow-van Deventer Model for Valuing Non-Maturity Deposits, Journal of Derivatives, Vol. 7,Fall, pp. 8-31

Jarrow, R.A., van Deveter, D.R. (1998): The arbitrage-free valuation and hedging of demand deposits and credit card loans, Journal of Banking and Finance, Vol. 22, pp. 249-272

Kalkbrener, M., Wiling, J. (2004): Risk management of non-maturing liabilities, Journal of Banking and Finance, Vol. 28, pp. 1547-1568

Kall, P., Mayer, J. (2010): Stochastic Linear Programming: Models, Theory, and Computation, 2nd ed., New York: Springer

Kahn, C., Pennacchi, G. and Sopranzetti, B. (1999): Bank Deposit Clustering: Theory and Empirical Evidence, Journal of Finance, Vol. 54, Dec., pp. 2185-2214

Kim, D.O. and Orphanides, A. (2005): Term Structure Estimation with Survey Data on Interest Rate Forecasts, Finance and Economics Discussion Series, Divisions of Research & Statistics and Monetary Affairs, Federal Reserve Board, Washington, D.C

Kutner, M.H., Nachtsheim, C.J., Neter, J., Li, W. (2005): Applied Linear Statistical Models, 5th ed., New York: McGraw-Hill/Irwin

Laurent, M.P. (2004): Non-Maturity Deposits with a Fidelity Premium, Working Paper, Solvay Business School, pp. 1-27

Laurini, M.P., Hotta, L.K. (2008): Bayesian Extensions to Diebold-Li Term Structure Model, Ibmec Working Papers wpe_122, Insper Working Paper, Insper Instituto de Ensino e Pesquisa

Llewellyn, D.T. (1999): The new Economics of Banking, Amsterdam: SUERF

Maes, K.,Timmermans, T. (2005): Measuring the Interest Rate Risk of Belgian Regulated Savings Deposits, National Bank of Belgium, Financial Stability Review, pp. 137-152

Mester, L.J., Saunders, A. (1995): When does the Prime Rate Change?, Journal of Banking and Finance, Vol. 19, pp. 743-764

Nawalkha, S.K., Beliaeva, N.A., Soto, M.G. (2007): Dynamic Term Structure Modeling: The fixed Income Valuation Course, Hoboken: Wiley

Nelson, C.R., Siegel, A.F. (1987): Parsimonious Modeling of Yield Curves, Journal of Business, Vol. 60, pp. 473-489

Neumark, D., Sharpe, S. (1995): Market Structure and the Nature of Price Rigidity: Evidence from the Market for Consumer Deposits, Quarterly Journal of Economics, Vol 107, pp. 657-680

Neumark, D., Sharpe, S. (1992): Market Structure and the Nature of Price Rigidity, Quarterly Journal of Economics, Vol. 429, pp. 657-680

Nyström, K. (2008): On deposit volumes and the valuation of non-maturing liabilities, Journal of Economic Dynamics & Control, Vol. 32, Iss. 3, pp. 709-756

O'Brien, J., Orphanides, A., Small, D. (1994): Estimating the Interest Rate Sensitivity of Liquid Retail Deposits, Proceedings of a Conference on Bank Structure and Competition, Chicago Federal Reserve Bank, pp. 400-435

Österreichische Nationalbank (2012): Banks' Business Structure, retrieved from http://www.oenb.at/en/stat_melders/datenangebot/finanzinst/kreditinstitute/geschaeftsstruktur/geschaeftsstruktur.jsp, last update 2012-03-30, accessed March 30, 2012

Office of Thrift Supervision, Department of the Treasury (1994): The OTS Net Portfolio Value Model, OTC

Office of Thrift Supervision, Department of the Treasury (2001): Net Portfolio Value Model, OTC

Paraschiv, F., Schürle, M. (2010): Modeling Client Rate and Volumes of Non-Maturing Accounts, Working Paper Series: Universität St. Gallen, pp. 1-28

Paraschiv, F., Frauendorfer, K. (2011): Modeling Client Rates and Volumes of the Swiss Savings Accounts, Working Paper Series: Universität St. Gallen

R Development Core Team (2008): R: A language and environment for statistical computing, R Foundation for Statistical Computing, Vienna, Austria. ISBN 3-900051-07-0, URL http://www.R-project.org

Rebonato, R. (2002): Modern Pricing of Interest-Rate Derivatives: The LIBOR Market Model and Beyond, Princeton: Princeton University Press

Rosen, R. (2002): What comes up must come down? Asymmetries and persistence in bank deposit rates, Journal of Financial Services Research, Vol 21, pp. 173-193

Schürle, M. (1998): Zinsmodelle in der stochastischen Optimierung, Bern: Haupt

Selvaggio, Robert (1996): Using the OAS Methodology to Value and Hedge Commercial Bank Retail Demand Deposit Premiums, Handbook of Asset/Liability Management, Fabbozi, F. and Knoishi, A. (eds.), pp. 363-373

Sharpe, W.F. (1966): Mutual Fund Performance, Journal of Business, Vol. 39, No. 1, Part 2: Supplement on Security Prices, pp. 119-138

Sheehan, R.G. (2004): Valuing Core Deposits, Department of Finance, University of Notre Dame, Notre Dame

Siede, H. (2000): Multi-Period Portfolio Optimization, Ph.D. Dissertation, University of St. Gallen, Bamberg: Difo-Druck

Svensson, L.E.O. (1994): Estimating and Interpreting Forward Interest Rates: Sweden 1992-1994, International Monetary Fund, Working Paper WP/94/114

Varadhan, R., Gilbert, P. (2009): BB: An R Package for Solving a Large System of Nonlinear Equations and for Optimizing a High-Dimensional Nonlinear Objective Function, Journal of Statistical Software, Vol. 32, No. 4, pp. 1-26

Vasicek, O. (1977): An Equilibrium Characterization of the Term Structure, Journal of Financial Economics, Vol. 5, No. 2, pp. 177-188

Venables, W.N., Ripley, B.D. (2002): Modern Applied Statistics with S, 4th ed., New York: Springer

Wilson, T.C. (1994): Optimal Values, Balance Sheet, Vol. 3, No. 3, pp. 13-20

Zanjani, M.K., Nourelfath, M., Aït-Kadi, D. (2010): A Multi-Stage Stochastic Programming Approach for Production Planning with Uncertainty in the Quality of Raw Materials and Demand, International Journal of Production Research, Vol 48, Issue 16, pp. 4701-4723

Appendix

Appendix A: Scenario Generation Vasicek Model

```
## Short Rate Scenarios for MSP ##

# Load Data From Estimation Procedure
load("*/Data/Market Rates/M_Rates_Params.RData")
# Load Stochastic Factor Scenarios
load("*/Data/MSP/Stochastic_Factors.RData")

# Parameters from Estimation Procedure
theta <- res$par[2]   # Long-Term Mean
sigma <- res$par[3]   # Standard Deviation of Increments
alpha <- res$par[1]    # Speed of Mean Reversion

# Current Market Rate at Simulation Starting Time
r0 <- euribor.data[150,2] # From Time-Series/Current Market Data

# Path Simulation
T <- 0.5    # Number of Years
m <- 6   # Number of Subintervals (Months)
dt <- T/m  # Time Delta between Subintervals
stages <- m # Number of Stages
n <- length(rand.scen[1,])^stages    # Number of Simulations

# Create Path Matrix (Each Column = One Path)
r <- matrix(nrow = n, ncol = stages+1)
# Set the Initial Rate of all Paths to Current Market Rate
r[,1] <- r0
# Vector Holding all Deltas of Interest Rates for Time t
dr.vec <- 1:n

# Scenario Set Selection
# Create A Vector of Random Numbers between 0 and 11
scen.sel <- round(runif(n=stages, min = -0.5, max = num.scen-0.5))

# Create Matrix Holding all Stochastic Factor Scenarios
stoch.mat <-  matrix(nrow = n, ncol = stages)
# Fill Matrix With the Relevant Stochastic Factor Scenarios
# For Each Stage k
for (k in 1:stages){
  stoch.mat[,k] <- rep(x = rep(x = rand.scen[1+2*scen.sel[k],],
    times = length(rand.scen[1,])^(k-1)), each = length(
    rand.scen[1,])^stages/length(rand.scen[1,])^k, times = 1)
}

# Calculate Change in Rate According to Vasicek SDE
# For Each Stage
for(i in 2:(m + 1)){
  dr.vec <- alpha*(theta - r[1:n,i-1])*dt +
    sigma*sqrt(dt)*stoch.mat[,i-1] # SDE
  # Save Discrete Path Evolution Values to Matrix
  r[1:n,i] <- r[1:n,i-1] + dr.vec
}

# Set all Negative Values to Zero
r[r < 0.0001] <- 0.0001

# Save Results
```

```
save(list = c("m", "n", "r", "res", "scen.sel"),
     file = "*/Data/Market Rates/Simulated_Rates.RData",
     precheck = TRUE)
# Clear Workspace
rm(list = objects())
```

Appendix B: Yield Curve Scenario Generation

```
## Yield Curve Scenario Generation (all paths) ##

# Load Outputs From Short Rate Simulation
load("*/Data/Market Rates/Simulated_Rates.RData")
# Maturities to be included in the Yield Curve
maturities<-c(1/12,0.25,1,5)

# Variable Definitions
# Vectors holding Parameters for Bond Price Equation
B.t.T <- c(length(maturities))
A.t.T <- c(length(maturities))
# Three Dimensional Bond Price Array
P.t.T <- array(0, c(n, m+1, length(maturities)))
# Three Dimensional Yield Data Array
yields <- array(0, c(n, m+1, length(maturities)))

# Calculation of Parameter Vectors A(t,T)&B(t,T)
for (i in 1:length(maturities)){
  B.t.T[i]<-(1-exp(-res$par[3]*maturities[i]))/res$par[3]
  A.t.T[i]<-((B.t.T[i]-maturities[i])*((res$par[3]^2*res$par[1]-
    res$par[2]^2/2))/ res$par[3]^2)-((res$par[2]^2*B.t.T[i]^2)/
    (4*res$par[3]))
  # Calculation of Bond Prices and Yields
  P.t.T[1:n,1:(m+1),i]<- exp(A.t.T[i]-B.t.T[i]*r[1:n,1:(m+1)])
  yields[1:n,1:(m+1),i]<- -log(P.t.T[1:n,1:(m+1),i])/maturities[i]
}

# Save Results
save(list = c("yields", "m", "n", "scen.sel", "maturities",
              "init.yc", "maturities1"),
     file = "*/Data/Market Rates/Simulated_YCs.RData",
     precheck = TRUE)
# Clear Workspace
rm(list = objects())
```

Appendix C: Estimation of a one-factor Vasicek model

```
## Vasicek Parameter Estimation - Maximum Likelihood ##

library(BB) # Load Package

# Read EURIBOR Rates
euribor.data  <-  read.table(file="*/Data/Market  Rates/Monthly  EURIBOR
Rates.csv", header=TRUE, sep =";", dec =",")
s.size <- 144 # Defining Sample Size
# Reducing Data to Sample Size
euribor.sample <- euribor.data[1:s.size,]

# Define Parameters and Assign Starting Values (subjective decision!)
theta.start <- mean(euribor.sample[,2])
sigma.start <- sd(euribor.sample[,2])
alpha.start <- 0.2
# Create a Vector holding the Parameters
params <- c(alpha.start, theta.start, sigma.start)

# Define Data Sample for Calibration (1M EURIBOR)
data.sample <- euribor.sample[,2]
del.t <- euribor.sample[2,1] - euribor.sample[1,1]
n <- length(data.sample) # Define Time Increments the Sample Features

# Negative Log-Likelihood Function
# See Formulas in Subchapter 3.1.3.
neg.log.likelihood <- function (parameters, data.s, d.t)
{ n <- length(data.sample) # Number of Observations in the Sample
  vari <- (parameters[3]^2)/(2*parameters[1])*
    (1 - exp(-2*parameters[1]*d.t))
  sum.vsquared <- 0
  for(i in 1:(n-1)){
    v <- (data.s[i+1] - (parameters[2] + (data.s[i]-parameters[2])*
      exp(-parameters[1]*d.t)))/sqrt(vari)
    sum.vsquared <- sum.vsquared + v^2
  }
  neg.log.likelihood <- (n-1)/2*log(2*pi) + (n-1)/2*log(vari) +
  0.5*sum.vsquared
}

# Constrained Non-Linear Minimization
# Define max. Iterations and Convergence Tolerance
specs <- list(maxit=3500, ftol=0.00001)
# Include Lower and Upper Bounds for Parameters
res<-spg(params, neg.log.likelihood, data.s = data.sample, d.t = del.t,
lower = c(0.001,0.001,0.001),
  upper = c(1.0,1.0,1.0), control = specs)
# Show Results
summary(res)

# Save Results
save(list = c("euribor.data", "res", "s.size"),
     file = "*/Data/Market Rates/M_Rates_Params.RData",
     precheck = TRUE)
# Unload Package
detach(package:BB)
# Clear Workspace
rm(list = objects())
```

Appendix D: Scenario Generation Client Rate Model

```
## Client Rate Scenario Generation ##

# Load Outputs From Yield Curve Simulation
load("*/Data/Market Rates/Simulated_YCs.RData")
# Load Data From Estimation Procedure
load("*/Data/Client Rates/C_Rates_Params.RData")
# Define Matrix Holding Client Rates
# n = Number of Simulations
# m = Number of Total Subintervals (Months)
cl.rate.mat <- matrix(ncol=m+1, nrow=n)

# Filling Client Rate Matrix
# Starting Value for all Paths is Current Client Rate
cl.rate.mat[,1]<- var.df[length(var.df[,1]),'client.rate']
# Matrix Holding Control variable
contr.var <- matrix(ncol=m, nrow=n)
# Matrix Holding Changes in Client Rate
d.cr.vec <- matrix(ncol=m, nrow=n)
# Factor Holding Changes Observed
cat.fac <- as.ordered(var.df[,'cl.rate.change'])

# For Each Stage, For all Paths
for(i in 2:(m+1)){
  # Regression Formula
  contr.var[1:n,i-1] <- polr.out$coefficients[1]*yields[1:n,i-1,1] +
    polr.out$coefficients[2]* (cl.rate.mat[1:n,i-1] - yields[1:n,i-1,1])
    #+ polr.out$coefficients[2]* (cl.rate.mat[i-1,1:n] - yields[i,1:n,6])
  # Check for Change Category
  # For Each Control Variable
  for (j in 1:n){
    # Check for Threshold (k = Number of Category)
    for  (k in 1:(nlevels(cat.fac)-1)){
      if (contr.var[j,i-1] < polr.out$zeta[k]) break
    }
    if (contr.var[j,i-1] > polr.out$zeta[nlevels(cat.fac)-1])
      k <- nlevels(cat.fac)
    # Save Jump
  d.cr.vec[j,i-1] <- levels(cat.fac)[k]
  # Calculate and Save Discrete Path Evolution Values to Matrix
  cl.rate.mat[j,i] <- max(0.0001,cl.rate.mat[j,i-1] +
    as.numeric(d.cr.vec[j,i-1]))
  }
}

# Save Results
save(list = "cl.rate.mat",
     file = "*/Data/Client Rates/Simulated_C_Rates.RData",
     precheck = TRUE)
# Clear Workspace
rm(list = objects())
```

Appendix E: Multinomial Ordered Logistic Regression Estimation

```
## Multinomial Ordered Logistic Regression Estimation ##

# Read Client Rate Data
cl.rates <- read.table(file="*/Data/Client Rates/Client Rates.csv",
  header = TRUE, sep = ";", dec = ",")
# Read Euribor Data (Short Term Rates)
swap.data <- read.table(file="*/Data/Market Rates/EURO Swap data.csv",
  header=TRUE, sep =";", dec =",")
# Read Swap Rate Data (Long Term Rates)
euribor.data  <-  read.table(file="*/Data/Market  Rates/Monthly  EURIBOR
Rates.
  csv", header=TRUE, sep =";", dec =",")
# Read Volume Data
volume.data <- read.table(file="*/Data/Volumes/Volume Data.csv",
  header = TRUE, sep = ";", dec = ",")

# Create Data Frame Holding the Variables
# Define Number of Lagged Short Term Rates (or Spreads) to be Used
st.lag.num <- 1
# Define Number of Lagged Long Term Rates (or Spreads) to be Used
lt.lag.num <- 1
# Define Common Number of Observations Used for all Samples
com.samp.size <- 30 # 30 (monthly) Observations
# Columns = Non-Exhaustive Collection of Explanatory Variables
# Rows = Number of Observations for Each Variable
var.df <- data.frame(st.rate = euribor.data[(st.lag.num+1):com.samp.size,
  2], st.lag1 = euribor.data[st.lag.num:(com.samp.size-1),2],
  lt.rate = swap.data[(st.lag.num+1):com.samp.size,7],
  lt.lag1 = swap.data[(st.lag.num):(com.samp.size-1),7],
  client.rate = cl.rates[(st.lag.num+1):com.samp.size,2],
  cl.rate.lag = cl.rates[st.lag.num:(com.samp.size-1),2],
  cl.rate.change = 0:(com.samp.size-st.lag.num-1),
  spr.st.lag1 = 0:(com.samp.size-st.lag.num-1),
  spr.lt.lag1 = 0:(com.samp.size-lt.lag.num-1))

# Attach Volume Time Series to Existing Data Frame of Variables
var.df <- cbind(var.df, NMA.Volumes = volume.data[(st.lag.num+1):
  com.samp.size,2], Vol.Changes = log(volume.data[(st.lag.num+1):
  com.samp.size,2]) - log(volume.data[st.lag.num:(com.samp.size-1)
  ,2]), vol.lag = volume.data[st.lag.num:(com.samp.size-1),2])

# Fill Client Rate Change Data
var.df[1:length(var.df[,'client.rate']),'cl.rate.change'] <-
  var.df[1:(length(var.df[,1])),'client.rate'] -
  var.df[1:length(var.df[,1]),'cl.rate.lag']

# Define specifications of Client Rate Change Categories
step.size <- 1/2000  # Jumps Occur in Multiples of Step Size
# Map Changes to Change Categories
# First Category
first.cat <- round(min(var.df[,'cl.rate.change'])*(1/step.size))/
  (1/step.size)
# Last Category
last.cat <- round(max(var.df[,'cl.rate.change'])*(1/step.size))/
  (1/step.size)
# Round to Closest Step
var.df[,'cl.rate.change'] <- round(var.df[,'cl.rate.change']*
  (1/step.size))/(1/step.size)
# Map Changes Outside of Category Range to Closest Category
var.df[var.df[,'cl.rate.change'] < first.cat,'cl.rate.change'] <-
```

```
  first.cat
var.df[var.df[,'cl.rate.change'] > last.cat,'cl.rate.change'] <- last.cat

# Fill (Lagged) Spread Data
# Short-Term Spread (Current Short-Term Rate - Last Client Rate)
var.df[1:length(var.df[,1]),'spr.st.lag1'] <- var.df[1:length(var.df[,1])
  , 'cl.rate.lag'] - var.df[1:length(var.df[,1]),'st.lag1']
# Long-Term Spread (Current Long-Term Rate - Last Client Rate)
var.df[1:length(var.df[,1]),'spr.lt.lag1'] <- var.df[1:length(var.df[,1])
  , 'cl.rate.lag'] - var.df[1:length(var.df[,1]),'lt.lag1']

# Estimation Function "polr" From MASS Package
library(MASS)
# Specify Optimization Parameters
specs<-list(maxit=1000)
# Define the Regression Formula, Method, and Data
polr.out <- polr(formula = as.ordered(cl.rate.change)  ~
  st.lag1 + spr.st.lag1, method="logistic",
  data = var.df, Hess=TRUE, control=specs)
# Show Output
summary(polr.out)
# In-sample Test
predict(polr.out)
as.ordered(var.df[,7])
summary(predict(polr.out))

# Save Results
save(list = c("var.df", "polr.out"),
     file = "*/Data/Client Rates/C_Rates_Params.RData",
     precheck = TRUE)
# Unload Package
detach(package:MASS)
# Clear Workspace
rm(list = objects())
```

Appendix F: Scenario Generation NMA Volumes Model

```
## Scenario Generation Volume Model ##

# Load Estimation Parameters
load("*/Data/Volumes/Volumes_Params.RData")
# Load Simulated Data
load("*/Data/Client Rates/Simulated_C_Rates.RData")
load("*/Data/Market Rates/Simulated_YCs.RData")
# Load Stochastic Factor Scenarios
load("*/Data/MSP/Stochastic_Factors.RData")

# Create and Fill Matrix for Dummy Variables
dum.var.mat <- matrix(data = c(rep(c(1,rep(0,12)),11),4),
  ,ncol = 12, nrow = m, byrow = TRUE)
# Input First Month in Data Series (Here July = 7)
start.month <- 7
# Rearrange Dummy Matrix to Beginn With Correct Month
# Create Auxiliary Vector With Correct Order of Months
aux.vec <- (-start.month + 2):(-start.month + 13)
aux.vec[aux.vec <= 0] <- aux.vec[aux.vec <= 0] + 12
# Use Auxiliary Vector to Create Corrected Matrix
dum.var.mat <- dum.var.mat[,aux.vec]

# Define Matrix Holding Simulated NMA Volumes
# n = Number of Simulations
# m = Number of Stages
vol.mat <- matrix(ncol = m+1, nrow = n)
# Define Vector Holding Changes in Volume
del.vol.vec <- 1:n

# Create Matrix Holding all Stochastic Factor Scenarios
stoch.mat <-  matrix(nrow = n, ncol = m)
# Fill Matrix With the Relevant Stochastic Factor Scenarios
# For Each Stage k
for (k in 1:m){
  stoch.mat[,k] <- rep(x = rep(x = rand.scen[2+2*scen.sel[k],], times =
    length(rand.scen[1,])^(k-1)), each = length(rand.scen[1,])^m
    /length(rand.scen[1,])^k, times = 1)
}
# Incorporate Autoregression in Stochastic Factors (5 Lags)
# Create Matrix Holding Last Five Residuals
res.mat      <-      matrix(data      =      rep(res.vol[(length(res.vol)-
4):length(res.vol)], each = n), nrow = n, ncol = 5)
# Attach Residuals to Error Term Matrix
aux.stoch.mat <- cbind(res.mat, stoch.mat)

# Check and Calculate Autoregression
if (length(autoreg.res$ar) == 0) break else {
  # For Each Stage k
  if (length(autoreg.res$ar) == 1){for (k in 1:m){
    stoch.mat[,k] <- stoch.mat[,k] + autoreg.res$ar * aux.stoch.mat[,k+4]
+
    autoreg.res$ar^2    *    aux.stoch.mat[,k+3]    +    autoreg.res$ar^3    *
aux.stoch.mat[,k+2] +
    autoreg.res$ar^4    *    aux.stoch.mat[,k+1]    +    autoreg.res$ar^5    *
aux.stoch.mat[,k]}
    }
  else {for (k in 1:m){
    stoch.mat[,k]     <-     stoch.mat[,k]     +     autoreg.res$ar[1]     *
aux.stoch.mat[,k+4] +
```

```
    autoreg.res$ar[2]   *   aux.stoch.mat[,k+4]+   autoreg.res$ar[1]^2   *
aux.stoch.mat[,k+3] +
    autoreg.res$ar[2]^2  *  aux.stoch.mat[,k+3]+  autoreg.res$ar[1]^3  *
aux.stoch.mat[,k+2] +
    autoreg.res$ar[2]^3  *  aux.stoch.mat[,k+2]+  autoreg.res$ar[1]^4  *
aux.stoch.mat[,k+1] +
    autoreg.res$ar[2]^4  *  aux.stoch.mat[,k+1]+  autoreg.res$ar[1]^5  *
aux.stoch.mat[,k] +
    autoreg.res$ar[2]^5 * aux.stoch.mat[,k]
    }
  }
}

# Define Vectors Holding Upper and Lower Volume Limits
min.vol.lim <- rep(0, times = m)
max.vol.lim <- rep(0, times = m)

# Calculate Upper and Lower Relative Limits for Scenarios
for (i in 1:m){
  for (k in i:length(var.df[,1])){
  min.vol.lim[i] <- min(min.vol.lim[i], var.df[k,"NMA.Volumes"]/
    var.df[k-(i-1),"vol.lag"] - 1)
  max.vol.lim[i] <- max(max.vol.lim[i], var.df[k,"NMA.Volumes"]/
    var.df[k-(i-1),"vol.lag"] - 1)
  }
}
# Define Multiplier for Percentage of Max Sample Rise/Decline
max.decl <- 2
max.rise <- 2

# Filling NMA Volume Matrix
# Starting Value for all Paths is Current NMA Volume
vol.mat[,1] <- var.df[length(var.df[,1]),'NMA.Volumes']
# For Each Subinterval(i), For all Paths
for(i in 2:(m+1)){
  del.vol.vec <- params.volumes[1] + params.volumes[2] * yields[,i-1,1] +
  params.volumes[3] * (cl.rate.mat[,i-1] - yields[,i-1,1]) +
  params.volumes[4] * dum.var.mat[i-1,6] + params.volumes[5] *
  dum.var.mat[i-1,7]
  del.vol.vec <- del.vol.vec * vol.mat[,i-1]  + stoch.mat[,i-1] *
    vol.mat[,i-1]
  # Save Volume Evolution Step to Output Matrix
  vol.mat[,i] <- vol.mat[,i-1] + del.vol.vec
}

for(i in 2:(m+1)){
  # Adjust Scenarios That Exceed Maximum Rise Limit
  vol.mat[vol.mat[,i] > vol.mat[1,1] + max.rise * max.vol.lim[i-1] *
    vol.mat[1,1],i] <- vol.mat[1,1] + max.rise * max.vol.lim[i-1] *
    vol.mat[1,1]
  # Adjust Scenarios That lie Below Maximum Decline Limit
  vol.mat[vol.mat[,i] < vol.mat[1,1] + max.decl * min.vol.lim[i-1] *
    vol.mat[1,1],i] <- vol.mat[1,1] + max.decl * min.vol.lim[i-1] *
    vol.mat[1,1]
}

# Save Overall Results
save(list = c("vol.mat", "cl.rate.mat", "yields"),
     file = "*/Data/MSP/Simulation_Result.RData",
     precheck = TRUE)

# Save Results
save(list = "vol.mat",
```

```
     file = "*/Data/Volumes/Sim_Volumes.RData",
     precheck = TRUE)
# Clear Workspace
rm(list = objects())
```

Appendix G: NMA Volume Model Estimation Step 1

```
## Linear Regression Model for NMA Volume ##

# Load Previous Results
load("*/Data/Client Rates/C_Rates_Params.RData")

# Create and Fill Matrix for Dummy Variables
dum.var.mat <- matrix(data=c(rep(c(rep(c(1,rep(0,12)),11),1),
  length(var.df[,1])/12)) ,ncol = 12, nrow = length(var.df[,1]),
  byrow = TRUE)
# Input First Month in Data Series (Here February = 2)
start.month <- 2
# Rearrange Dummy Matrix to Beginn With Correct Month
# Create Auxiliary Vector With Correct Order of Months
aux.vec <- (-start.month + 2):(-start.month + 13)
aux.vec[aux.vec <= 0] <- aux.vec[aux.vec <= 0] + 12
# Use Auxiliary Vector to Create Corrected Matrix
dum.var.mat <- dum.var.mat[,aux.vec]
# Create Data Frame Holding Dummy Variables
dum.var.df <- data.frame(Jan = dum.var.mat[,1], Feb = dum.var.mat[,2],
  Mar = dum.var.mat[,3], Apr = dum.var.mat[,4], May = dum.var.mat[,5],
  Jun = dum.var.mat[,6], Jul = dum.var.mat[,7], Aug = dum.var.mat[,8],
  Sep = dum.var.mat[,9], Oct = dum.var.mat[,10], Nov = dum.var.mat[,11],
  Dec = dum.var.mat[,12])
# Combine Data Frames
var.df <- cbind(var.df,dum.var.df)

# Define Names of Variables Used in Regression Function
variables.used <- c("Vol.Changes", "st.lag1", "spr.st.lag1", "Jun",
  "Jul")
#variables.used <- c("Vol.Changes", "client.rate")
# Perform OLS Regression
ols.out <- lm(formula(paste(variables.used[1], paste(variables.used
  [2:length(variables.used)], collapse = " + "),sep = " ~ ")),
  data = var.df)
# Show Results
summary(ols.out)
# Save Estimated Coefficients to Vector
params.volumes <- ols.out$coef[1:length(ols.out$coef)]

# Check for Autocorrelation in Residuals
autoreg.res <- ar(ols.out$residuals, aic = TRUE)
# Show Results of Autoregression Check
autoreg.res$order
autoreg.res$ar
# Show Autocorrelation Graph
acf( ols.out$residuals)

# Calculation of a Standard Deviation for the 2nd Stochastic Factor
# Standard Deviation of the Residuals
sd.res.vol <- sd(residuals(ols.out))

# Residuals
res.vol <- residuals(ols.out)

# Save Volume at Time t = -1 (for MSP constraints)
vol.past <- var.df[length(var.df[,1]), "vol.lag"]
# Save Results
save(list = c("vol.past"),
   file = "*/Data/Volumes/Volumes t minus 1.RData",
   precheck = TRUE)
```

```
# Save Results
save(list = c("variables.used", "autoreg.res",
  "sd.res.vol", "var.df", "params.volumes", "res.vol"),
   file = "*/Data/Volumes/Volumes_Params.RData",
   precheck = TRUE)
# Clear Workspace
rm(list = objects())
```

Appendix H: NMA Volume Model Estimation Autocorrelation Adjustment

```
## Linear Regression Model for NMA Volume with Autoregressive Errors ##

# Load Outcome From Linear Regression
load("*/Data/Volumes/Volumes_Params.RData")
# Number of Dummy Variables Used
num.dum <- 0
# Create Vector Holding Explanatory Variables without Dummy Variables
variables.adj <- matrix(ncol = length(variables.used) - num.dum,
  nrow = length(var.df[,1]) - autoreg.res$order)

# Adjust Variables for Autoregression
for (i in 1:(length(variables.used[])-num.dum)){
  x <- var.df[(1+autoreg.res$order):length(var.df[,1]),variables.used[i]]
  for (k in 1:autoreg.res$order){
  x <- x - autoreg.res$ar[k]*var.df[(1+autoreg.res$order-k):
    (length(var.df[,1]) - k),variables.used[i]]
  }
  variables.adj[,i] <- x
}

# Create Data Frame with Adjusted Variables
variables.adj <- data.frame(variables.adj)
# Fill Original Dummy Variables
variables.adj <- cbind(variables.adj, var.df[(1+autoreg.res$order):
  length(var.df[,1]),variables.used[(length(variables.used)-num.dum):
  length(variables.used)]])
# Define Variable Names
names(variables.adj) <- variables.used
# Perform OLS Regression
ols.out <- lm(formula(paste(variables.used[1], paste(variables.used
  [2:length(variables.used)], collapse = " + "),sep = " ~ ")),
  data = variables.adj)
# Show Results
summary(ols.out)

# Variable Holding Intercept Adjustment Coefficient
int.adj <- 1
# Calculate Intercept Adjustment Coefficient
for (k in 1:autoreg.res$order){
  int.adj <- int.adj - autoreg.res$ar[k]
}
# Save Estimated (Adjusted) Coefficients to Vector
params.volumes <- c(ols.out$coef[1]/int.adj,
  ols.out$coef[2:length(ols.out$coef)])

# Re-Check for Autocorrelation
check.res <- ar(residuals(ols.out), aic = TRUE, demean = FALSE)
# Show Results of Autoregression Check
check.res$order
check.res$ar

# Calculation of a Standard Deviation for the 2nd Stochastic Factor
# Standard Deviation of the Residuals
sd.res.vol <- sd(residuals(ols.out))

# Save Results
save(list = c("variables.used", "params.volumes", "var.df",
  "sd.res.vol", "autoreg.res", "check.res", "res.vol" ),
     file = "*/Data/Volumes/Volumes_Params.RData",
     precheck = TRUE)
```

```
# Clear Workspace
rm(list = objects())
```

Appendix I: Stochastic Factor Scenario Generation

```
## Stochastic Factor Scenario Generation and Probabilities ##

# Approximate Stochastic Factor Outcomes by Multinomial Distribution
n <- 2 # Number of Distributions (Stochastic Factors)
m <- 1 # Generate m+n Over m Scenarios per Scenario Set
# Create and Fill Transformation Matrix
trans.m <- matrix(ncol = n+1, nrow = n+1)
for (i in 0:n){
  for (j in 0:n){
    if (i == 0) trans.m[i+1,j+1] <- (1/(n+1))^(1/2) else {
      if (i > 0 & j == i-1) trans.m[i+1,j+1] <- -((n-i+1)/(n-i+2))^(1/2)
      else {if (i > 0 & j >= i) trans.m[i+1,j+1] <- (1/((n-i+1)*(n-i+2))
        )^(1/2) else {trans.m[i+1,j+1] <- 0}
      }
    }
  }
}
# Create Vector Holding Possible Outcomes
out.binom <- matrix(ncol = n+1, nrow = choose(n+m, m))
# Load Package for Creating Permutations
library(gtools)
# Creating all Possible Cominations of Integers From 0:n
perm <- permutations(n = n+1, r =  n+1
  , v = c(0:n), repeats.allowed=TRUE)
# Delete all Rows not Summing up to n
out.binom <- perm[rowSums(perm)== m, , drop=FALSE]

# Load Variance of Residuals
load("*/Data/Volumes/Volumes_Params.RData")
# Create Covariance Matrix (With Standard Deviations in the Diagonal)
cov.mat <- matrix(data = 0, ncol = n, nrow = n)
# Fill Covariance Matrix
for (i in 1:n){
  if (i < n) cov.mat[i,i] <- 1 else cov.mat[i,i] <- sd.res.vol
}
# Create and Fill Vector Holding Expected Values for Random Variables
# Expected Values all Zero per Assumption
exp.val <- matrix(data = rep(0,n), ncol = choose(n+m, m), nrow = n)

# Create Vector Holding Orthogonalized Distributions
ortho <- matrix(ncol = length(out.binom[1,]), nrow =
  length(out.binom[,1]))
# Create Rotation Matrix (Identity Matrix)
rot.mat <- diag(n+1)

# Define Number of Scenario Sets
num.scen <- 12
# Create Matrix Holding Different Final Scnenario Sets
rand.scen <- matrix(nrow = n*num.scen , ncol = choose(n+m, m))

for (k in 1:num.scen){
  rot.angle <- 120/num.scen*k
  # Fill Rotation Matrix
  for (i in 2:n){
    for (j in 2:(n+1)){
      rot.mat[i,i] <- cos(rot.angle*pi/180)
      rot.mat[j,j] <- cos(rot.angle*pi/180)
      rot.mat[j,i] <- -sin(rot.angle*pi/180)
      rot.mat[i,j] <- sin(rot.angle*pi/180)
    }
```

```
  }

  # Multiply Transformation Matrix with Scenarios (Orthogonalize)
  for (l in 1:length(out.binom[,1])){
    ortho[l,] <- (rot.mat %*% trans.m) %*% out.binom[l,]
  }
  # Create Matrix Holding Disretized Random Variables
  disc.ran <-  matrix(ncol = length(out.binom[1,]), nrow =
    length(out.binom[,1]))
  # Divide by Standard Deviation to get Discrete Random Variables
  disc.ran <- ((n+1)/m)^(0.5)*ortho

  # Create Approximation for Multivariate Normal Distribution
  rand.scen[(((k-1)*2)+1):(((k-1)*2)+2),] <-
  (cov.mat %*% t(disc.ran[,2:(n+1)])) + exp.val
}

# Probability Calculation
# Define Vector Holding Probabilities
probs <- 1:choose(n+m, m)
# For Each Scenario Point
for (i in 1:choose(n+m, m)){
  probs[i] <- factorial(m)/prod(factorial(out.binom[i,]))*(1/(n+1))^m
}

# Save Results
save(list = c("rand.scen", "num.scen", "probs"),
     file = "*/Data/MSP/Stochastic_Factors.RData",
     precheck = TRUE)
# Unload Package
detach(package:gtools)
# Clear Workspace
rm(list = objects())
```

Appendix J: Scenario Probabilities

```
## Probability Matrices for Scenario Generation ##

# Load Stochastic Factor Scenarios
load("*/Data/MSP//Stochastic_Factors.RData")
# Load Stage and Scenario Numbers
load("*/Data/Market Rates/Simulated_Rates.RData")

# Define Matrix Holding Probabilities per Stage per Scenario
cond.prob.mat <- matrix(ncol = m, nrow= n)
# Define Matrix Holding Unconditional Probabilities
prob.mat <- matrix(ncol = m+1, nrow= n)

# Fill all (unconditional) Probabilities per Stage
for (k in 1:m){
  cond.prob.mat[,k] <- rep(x = rep(x = probs, times =
    length(probs)^(k-1)), each = length(probs)^m
    /length(probs)^k, times = 1)
}

# Calculate Conditional Probability Matrix
# Fill First Column with 1 (Probability of Current Observation)
prob.mat[,1] <- 1
# Fill Second Column With (Unconditional) Probabilities
prob.mat[,2] <- cond.prob.mat[,1]
# Fill all Conditional Probabilities per Stage
for (k in 2:m){
  prob.mat[,k+1] <- prob.mat[,k] * cond.prob.mat[,k]
}
# Check Sum of Final Probabilities (Must Equal 1)
sum(prob.mat[,7])

# Save Results
save(list = c("prob.mat", "m", "probs", "cond.prob.mat"),
     file = "*/Data/MSP/Scenario_Probabilites.RData",
     precheck = TRUE)
# Clear Workspace
rm(list = objects())
```

Appendix K: Initial Portfolio Cash Flows

```
## Inital Portfolio Cashflows and Amounts ##

# Load MSP Data
load("*/Data/Market Rates/Simulated_YCs.RData")
# Load Volume at Time t = -1
load("*/Data/Volumes/Volumes t minus 1.RData")
# Read Euribor Data (Short Term Rates)
swap.data <- read.table(file=
  "*Data/Market Rates/Monthly EURO Swap data.csv",
  header=TRUE, sep =";", dec =",")
# Read Swap Rate Data (Long Term Rates)
euribor.data <- read.table(file=
  "*/Data/Market Rates/Monthly EURIBOR Rates.csv",
  header=TRUE, sep =";", dec =",")
# Load Sample Size Data
load("*/Data/Market Rates/M_Rates_Params.RData")

# Load Initial Portfolio Weights (External Input)
init.weights <- c(0.3,0,0.1,0, 0, 0.6, 0, 0)

# Scale Maturities to Months
maturities.months <- maturities * 12

# Create Matrix Holding Monthly Weights of Contracts
month.weights.init <- matrix(data = 0, ncol = maturities.months
  [length(maturities.months)], nrow = length(maturities.months)+1)

# Calculate Actual Portfolio Positions
for (i in 1:length(init.weights)) {
  for (k in 1:maturities.months[i]){
    month.weights.init[i, 1:k] <- init.weights[i]/maturities.months[i]
  }
}
# Add a Sum of Amounts in Each Bucket
month.weights.init[length(maturities.months)+1,] <-
  colSums(month.weights.init[1:length(maturities.months),])

# Create Matrix Holding Past Rates
past.rates <- matrix(data = 0, ncol = maturities.months[
  length(maturities.months)], nrow = length(maturities))
# Fill Matrix
for (i in 1:length(maturities)) {
  if (sum(maturities[i] == c (1/12, 0.25, 0.5, 1)) > 0){
  past.rates[i,1:maturities.months[i]] <- euribor.data[
    (s.size-maturities.months[i]+1):s.size,
    sum((maturities[i] == c (1/12, 0.25, 0.5, 1))*1:4)+1]
  } else {
  past.rates[i,1:maturities.months[i]] <- swap.data[
    (s.size-maturities.months[i]+1):s.size, maturities[i]+2]
  }
}

# Create Matrix Holding Future Cash Flows (in % of Nominal Amount)
init.icf <- matrix(data = 0, ncol = past.rates[1,], nrow =
  past.rates[,1])
# Fill Matrix
init.icf <-  (past.rates/12)

# Create Matrix Holding Future Cash Flows (Absolute Amount)
init.ncf <- matrix(data = 0, ncol = past.rates[1,], nrow =
```

```
  past.rates[,1])
# Fill Matrix
init.ncf <-  init.icf * month.weights.init[1:length(past.rates[,1]),]*
  vol.past

# Create Matrix Holding Future Weights From Inital Portfolio
month.weights.init.dev <- matrix(data = 0, nrow = length(
  month.weights.init[,1]) , ncol = length(month.weights.init[1,]))
# Fill Array
month.weights.init.dev <- month.weights.init * vol.past

# Create Vector Holding Current Yield Curve
current.yc <- 1:length(maturities)
# Fill Vector With Current Maturities
for (i in 1:length(maturities)) {
  if (sum(maturities[i] == c (1/12, 0.25, 0.5, 1)) > 0){
  current.yc[i] <- euribor.data[s.size, sum((maturities[i] ==
     c(1/12, 0.25, 0.5, 1))*1:4)+1]
  } else {
  current.yc[i] <- swap.data[s.size, maturities[i]+2]
  }
}

# Save Results
save(list = c("init.ncf", "month.weights.init",
  "month.weights.init.dev"),
  file = "*/Data/Static Model/cash flows initial potfolio first.RData",
  precheck = TRUE)
# Clear Workspace
rm(list = objects())
```

Appendix L: Objective Function Vector

```
## Generate Objective Function Coefficient Vector ##

# Load Scenarios
load("*/Data/MSP/Simulation_Result.RData")
# Load Scenario Probabilities
load("*/Data/MSP/Scenario_Probabilites.RData")
# Load Yield Curve Data
load("*/Data/Market Rates/Simulated_YCs.RData")

# Define Parameters for the MSP
# Number of Stages
stages <- 6
# Number of Scenarios per Stage
scen <- length(probs)
# Define Varible Holding NUmber of Future States of the World
num.states <- 0
# Calculate Number of Future States of the World
for (i in 0:stages){
  num.states <- num.states + scen^i
}
# Define Vector Holding Probabilites
prob.vec <- 1:num.states
# Define Auxiliary Variable
aux <- 0
# Fill Vector With Probabilites
for (i in 1:stages){
  aux <- aux + scen^(i-1)
  prob.vec[(aux+1):((aux+1)+scen^(i)-1)] <- prob.mat[seq(from = 1,
  by = scen^(m-i), length.out = scen^i ),i+1]
}

# Adjusting Probabiities to get a sum of 1
prob.vec <- prob.vec/sum(prob.vec)

# Generate Vector of Coefficients for Objective Function
obj.fun <- c(rep(0,times = num.states*length(maturities)),
  rep(0,num.states),prob.vec)

# Export Outcome to .csv-File
write.csv2(obj.fun,
file="*/Data/MSP/Objective Function Vector.csv")

# Save Results
save(list = c("stages", "scen", "num.states", "obj.fun", "m",
     "maturities"), file = "*/Data/MSP/Objective_Function.RData",
     precheck = TRUE)
# Clear Workspace
rm(list = objects())
```

Appendix M: Right Hand Side Vector

```
## Generate Right Hand Side Vector of Constraints ##

# Load Parameter
load("*/Data/MSP/Objective_Function.RData")
# Load Initial Portfolio Cashflows
load("*/Data/Static Model/cash flows initial potfolio first.RData")
# Load Scenarios
load("*/Data/MSP/Simulation_Result.RData")
# Load Volume at Time t = -1
load("*/Data/Volumes/Volumes t minus 1.RData")
# Load Yield Curve Data
load("*/Data/Market Rates/Simulated_YCs.RData")
# Read Volume Data
volume.data <- read.table(file="*/Data/Volumes/Volume Data.csv",
  header = TRUE, sep = ";", dec = ",")

# Define Minimum Amounts in First Bucket (Max Outflow in the Past)
# Create Variable Holding Minimum Amount in the Past
max.out.past <- 0
# Calculate Maximum Outflow in the Past
for (i in 2:length(volume.data[,2])){
  max.out.past <- max(volume.data[i-1,2]/volume.data[i,2]-1,
    max.out.past)
}
#Create Vector Holding Minimum Amount for Each Stage
min.weight <- 0:stages
# Fill Vector With Maximum Outflows
min.weight[1] <- max.out.past
for (i in 1:stages){
  min.weight[i+1] <- max(max(vol.mat[,i]/vol.mat[,i+1]-1),
    min.weight[1:i])
}

# Constraint Equations per Scenario per Stage
constr.num <- 4
# (Non-Interest) Servicing Cost of the Account (per Year)
sc <- 0.0160

# Create Matrix Holding RHS of the Constraints
rhs.vec <- 1:(num.states*constr.num)
# Create Vector Holding Volume Scenarios
vol.vec <- 1:num.states
# Define Auxiliary Variable
aux <- 0
# Fill Vector Holding Volume Scenarios
for (i in 1:stages){
  aux <- aux + scen^(i-1)
  vol.vec[(aux+1):((aux+1)+scen^(i)-1)] <- vol.mat[seq(from = 1,
  by = scen^(m-i), length.out = scen^i ),i+1]
}
vol.vec[1] <- vol.mat[1,1]
aux <- 0

# Attach t - 1 Volume to Volume Vector
vol.vec <- c(vol.past, vol.vec)

write.csv2(vol.vec,
file="*/Data/Volumes/vol.vec.csv")

# Create Vector Holding Client Rate Scenarios
```

```
cl.vec <- 1:num.states
# Fill Vector Holding Client Rate Scenarios
for (i in 1:stages){
  aux <- aux + scen^(i-1)
  cl.vec[(aux+1):((aux+1)+scen^(i)-1)] <- cl.rate.mat[seq(from = 1,
  by = scen^(m-i), length.out = scen^i ),i+1]
}
cl.vec[1] <- cl.rate.mat[1,1]
# Define Auxiliary Variable (Representing Stage Number)
aux <- 0
# Is a Ratio of the Current Scenario Number Over the
# Maximum Number of Scenarios at the Current Stage
aux1<-0

# Calculate RHS Values
for (i in 1:(length(rhs.vec)/constr.num)){
  # Volume Constraints
  rhs.vec[1+(constr.num-1)*(i-1)] <- vol.vec[i+1] - sum(
  month.weights.init.dev[length(month.weights.init.dev[,1]), (aux+2):
  length(month.weights.init.dev[1,])])
  # Investment Policy Constraints
  if (aux == 0) {rhs.vec[2+(constr.num-1)*(i-1)] <- vol.vec[i+1] -
  vol.vec[i] + sum(month.weights.init.dev[length(month.weights.init[,1]),
  aux+1])} else
  {if (aux == 1) {rhs.vec[2+(constr.num-1)*(i-1)] <- vol.vec[i+1] -
    vol.vec[2] + sum(month.weights.init.dev[length(month.weights.init[,
    1]), aux+1])} else
      {aux1 <- ((i-sum(scen^(0:(aux-1))))/scen^aux)
      if (as.integer(aux1*scen^(aux-1)) < aux1*scen^(aux-1))
      {rhs.vec[2+(constr.num-1)*(i-1)] <- vol.vec[i+1] - vol.vec[
      sum(scen^c(0:(aux-2)))+ as.integer(aux1*scen^(aux-1))+2] + sum(
      month.weights.init.dev[length(month.weights.init[,1]), aux+1])}
      else {rhs.vec[2+(constr.num-1)*(i-1)] <- vol.vec[i+1] - vol.vec[
      sum(scen^c(0:(aux-2)))+ as.integer(aux1*scen^(aux-1))+1] + sum(
      month.weights.init.dev[length(month.weights.init[,1]), aux+1])}
      }
  }
  # Minimum Weight Constraints (Only Shortest Time Bucket)
  rhs.vec[3+(constr.num-1)*(i-1)] <- -min.weight * vol.vec[i+1] +
  sum(month.weights.init.dev[1:(length(month.weights.init[,1])-1),aux+2])
  # Auxiliary Constraint NMA Margin
  rhs.vec[num.states*(constr.num-1)+1+(i-1)] <- vol.vec[i+1] *
  -(cl.vec[i] + sc)/12 + sum(init.ncf[,(aux+2):length(init.ncf[1,])])
  # Calculating Auxiliary Variable (Representing Stage Number)
  if (aux == 0) aux <- aux + 1 else
  if (as.integer((i-sum(scen^(0:(aux-1))))/(scen^aux)) ==
  (i-sum(scen^(0:(aux-1))))/(scen^aux)) aux <- aux + 1
}

# Save Results
save(list = c("rhs.vec", "yields", "m", "constr.num", "num.states",
  "scen", "stages", "maturities"),
  file = "*/Data/MSP/Constraints Right Hand Side.RData",
  precheck = TRUE)
# Clear Workspace
rm(list = objects())
```

Appendix N: Left Hand Side Matrix

```
## Generate Left-Hand Side Matrix for Constraints ##

# Load Parameter
load("*/Data/MSP/Constraints Right Hand Side.RData")

# Create Matrix Holding Left Hand Side of Constraints
lhs.mat <- matrix(data = 0, nrow = num.states*constr.num,
  ncol = num.states*length(maturities) + 2*num.states)
# Define Auxiliary Variables
# Stands for the Stage of the Current Scenario
aux <- 0
# Is a Ratio of the Current Scenario Number Over the
# Maximum Number of Scenarios at the Current Stage
aux1 <- 0
# Create Matrix Holding Yield Curve Scenarios
yc.mat <- matrix(data = 0, nrow = num.states, ncol=length(maturities))
# Fill Matrix Holding Yield Curve Scenarios
for (i in 1:stages){
  aux <- aux + scen^(i-1)
  yc.mat[(aux+1):((aux+1)+scen^(i)-1),] <- yields[seq(from = 1,
  by = scen^(m-i), length.out = scen^i ),i+1,]
}
yc.mat[1,] <- yields[1,1,]
aux <- 0

# Calculate LHS Values
for (i in 1:(length(rhs.vec)/constr.num)){
  # Volume Constraints
  for (k in 0:aux){
    if (k == 0) {lhs.mat[1+(constr.num-1)*(i-1),(1 + (i-1)*
    length(maturities)):(i*length(maturities))]<- 1} else
    {x <- k < maturities[] * 12
    if (k == aux) {lhs.mat[1+(constr.num-1)*(i-1), (length(maturities) +
      1-sum(x)):length(maturities)] <- 1} else
      {aux1 <- ((i-sum(scen^(0:(aux-1))))/scen^aux)
      if (as.integer(aux1*scen^(aux-k)) < aux1*scen^(aux-k)) {
        lhs.mat[1+(constr.num-1)*(i-1),
        (sum(scen^c(0:(aux-k-1)))*length(maturities) +
        as.integer(aux1*scen^(aux-k)+1) *
        length(maturities)+1-sum(x)):(sum(scen^c(0:(aux-k-1)))*
        length(maturities) + as.integer(aux1*scen^(aux-k)+1) *
        length(maturities))]<- 1} else
        lhs.mat[1+(constr.num-1)*(i-1), (sum(scen^c(0:(aux-k-1)))*
        length(maturities) + as.integer(aux1*scen^(aux-k)) *
        length(maturities)+1-sum(x)) :(sum(scen^c(0:(aux-k-1)))*
        length(maturities) + as.integer(aux1*scen^(aux-k)) *
        length(maturities))]<- 1
      }
    }
  }
  # Investment Policy Constraints
  for (k in 0:aux){
    if (k == 0) {lhs.mat[2+(constr.num-1)*(i-1), (1 + (i-1)*
      length(maturities)):(i*length(maturities))] <- 1} else
      if (sum(k == maturities[] * 12)>0) {
        if (k == aux) {lhs.mat[2+(constr.num-1)*(i-1),
          which.max(k == maturities[] * 12)] <- -1} else
          {aux1 <- ((i-sum(scen^(0:(aux-1))))/scen^aux)
          if (as.integer(aux1*scen^(aux-k)) < aux1*scen^(aux-k)){
            lhs.mat[2+(constr.num-1)*(i-1), sum(scen^c(0:(aux-k-1))) *
```

```
          length(maturities) + as.integer(aux1*scen^(aux-k)) *
          length(maturities)+ which.max(k == maturities[] * 12)]<- -1}
          else {
          lhs.mat[2+(constr.num-1)*(i-1), sum(scen^c(0:(aux-k-1))) *
          length(maturities) + (as.integer(aux1*scen^(aux-k))-1) *
          length(maturities) + which.max(k == maturities[] * 12)]<- -1
        }
      }
    }
  }

# Minimum Weight Constraints (Only Shortest Time Bucket)
for (k in 0:aux){
  if (k == 0) {lhs.mat[3+(constr.num-1)*(i-1), 1 + (i-1)*
    length(maturities)]<- -1} else
    if (sum(k+1 == maturities[] * 12)>0) {
      {if (k == aux) {lhs.mat[3+(constr.num-1)*(i-1),
        which.max(k+1 == maturities[] * 12)]<- -1} else
        {aux1 <- ((i-sum(scen^(0:(aux-1))))/scen^aux)
        if (as.integer(aux1*scen^(aux-k)) < aux1*scen^(aux-k)) {
        lhs.mat[3+(constr.num-1)*(i-1), sum(scen^c(0:(aux-k-1)))*
        length(maturities) + as.integer(aux1*scen^(aux-k)) *
        length(maturities)+ which.max(k+1 == maturities[]
         * 12)]<- -1} else {
        lhs.mat[3+(constr.num-1)*(i-1), (sum(scen^(0:(aux-k-1))) *
        length(maturities) + (as.integer(aux1*scen^(aux-k))-1) *
        length(maturities)+ which.max(k+1 == maturities[] * 12))]<- -1
        }
      }
    }
  }
}
# Auxiliary Constraint NMA Margin
lhs.mat[num.states*(constr.num-1)+i,length(lhs.mat[1,])- num.states *
  2+ i] <- 1
for (k in 0:aux){
  if (k == 0) {lhs.mat[num.states*(constr.num-1)+i, ((i-1) *
  length(maturities)+1):(i*length(maturities))] <- -yc.mat[i,]/12} else
  {x <- k < maturities[] * 12
    if (k == aux) {lhs.mat[num.states*(constr.num-1)+i,(1 +
    length(maturities) - sum(x)): length(maturities)] <-
    -yc.mat[i,x]/12} else {
      aux1 <- ((i-sum(scen^(0:(aux-1))))/scen^aux)
      if (as.integer(aux1*scen^(aux-k)) < aux1*scen^(aux-k)) {
      lhs.mat[num.states*(constr.num-1)+i, (sum(scen^c(0:(aux-k-1))) *
      length(maturities) + 1 + (as.integer(aux1*scen^(aux-k))+1) *
      length(maturities) - sum(x)):(sum(scen^(0:(aux-k-1))) *
      length(maturities) + (as.integer(aux1*scen^(aux-k))+1) *
      length(maturities))]<- -yc.mat[i,x]/12} else
      {lhs.mat[num.states*(constr.num-1)+i, (sum(scen^c(0:(aux-k-1))) *
      length(maturities) + 1 + as.integer(aux1*scen^(aux-k)) *
      length(maturities) - sum(x)):(sum(scen^(0:(aux-k-1))) *
      length(maturities) + as.integer(aux1*scen^(aux-k)) *
      length(maturities))] <- -yc.mat[i,x]/12}
    }
  }
}
# Calculating Auxiliary Variable (Representing Stage Number)
if (aux == 0) aux <- aux + 1 else
if (as.integer((i-sum(scen^(0:(aux-1))))/(scen^aux)) ==
(i-sum(scen^(0:(aux-1))))/(scen^aux)) aux <- aux + 1
}
```

```
# Create Matrix Holding Auxiliary Constraints
aux.mat <- matrix(data = 0, nrow = 2*num.states,
  ncol = num.states*length(maturities) + 2*num.states)
# Define Weight for Upward Deviance
dev.up <- 0
# Define Weight for Downward Deviance
dev.down <- 1

# Fill Matrix Holding Auxiliary Constraints
for (i in 1:num.states){
  aux.mat[i,length(lhs.mat[1,])- num.states + i] <- -1
  aux.mat[i,length(lhs.mat[1,])- 2*num.states + i] <- - dev.down
  aux.mat[i+num.states,length(lhs.mat[1,])- num.states + i] <- -1
  aux.mat[i+num.states,length(lhs.mat[1,])- 2*num.states + i] <- dev.up
}
# Combine Matrices
lhs.mat <- rbind(lhs.mat, aux.mat)

# Create Right Hand Side Extension for Auxiliary Constraints
# Create a Vector of Zeros
zer.vec <- rep(0, 2*num.states)
# Combine RHS Vector With Zero Vector
rhs.vec <- c(rhs.vec,zer.vec)

# Create Vector of Operators for Constraint Equations
op.vec <- 1:length(lhs.mat[,1])
# Fill Vector of Operators
op.vec[1:((constr.num-1)*num.states)] <- rep(c("==","==","<="),
  times = (constr.num-1)*num.states)
op.vec[((constr.num-1)*num.states+1):(constr.num*num.states)] <- "=="
op.vec[(num.states * constr.num + 1):length(op.vec)] <- "<="

write.csv2(lhs.mat,
file="*/Data/MSP/Constraints Left Hand Side.csv")
write.csv2(rhs.vec,
file="*/Data/MSP/Constraints Right Hand Side.csv")
write.csv2(op.vec,
file="*/Data/MSP/Operators.csv")

# Save Results
save(list = c("lhs.mat", "rhs.vec", "op.vec"),
     file = "*/Data/MSP/Constraints Left Hand Side.RData",
     precheck = TRUE)
# Clear Workspace
rm(list = objects())
```

Appendix O: Solving the Multistage Stochastic Program

```
## Solve Multistage Stochastic Program ##

# Load Objective Function
load("*/Data/MSP/Objective_Function.RData")
# Load Constraints
load("*/Data/MSP/Constraints Left Hand Side.RData")

# Load Solver (R-GLPK)
library(Rglpk)

# Define Bounds on Decision Variables
bounds <- list(lower = list(ind = c((num.states*length(maturities)+1):
  length(lhs.mat[1,])), val = c(rep(-100,times = 2*num.states))),
  upper = list(ind = c(1:length(lhs.mat[1,])), val = c(rep(1000, times=
  length(lhs.mat[1,])))))

# Solve Linear Program
final.solution <- Rglpk_solve_LP(obj = obj.fun, mat = lhs.mat, dir =
  op.vec, rhs = rhs.vec, max=FALSE, verbose=TRUE, bounds = bounds)
final.solution

write.csv2(c(final.solution$solution[1:6], final.solution$optimum),
file="*/Data/MSP/RGLPK Solution Variables.csv")

# Save Results
save(list = c("final.solution"),
     file = "*/Data/Final_Outcome.RData",
     precheck = TRUE)
# Clear Workspace
rm(list = objects())
```

MIX
Papier aus verantwortungsvollen Quellen
Paper from responsible sources
FSC® C105338

If you have any concerns about our products,
you can contact us on
ProductSafety@springernature.com

In case Publisher is established outside the EU,
the EU authorized representative is:
Springer Nature Customer Service Center GmbH
Europaplatz 3, 69115 Heidelberg, Germany

Printed by Libri Plureos GmbH
in Hamburg, Germany